HAUNTED POTOMAC RIVER VALLEY

HAUNTED POTOMAC RIVER VALLEY

DAVID W. THOMPSON

Haunted America

Published by Haunted America
A Division of The History Press
Charleston, SC
www.historypress.com

First published 2021

Manufactured in the United States

ISBN 9781467147781

Library of Congress Control Number: 2021937195

Notice: The information in this book is true and complete to the best of our knowledge. It is offered without guarantee on the part of the author or The History Press. The author and The History Press disclaim all liability in connection with the use of this book.

I dedicate this to the all the friends who influenced me for so many years and inspired my writing, especially the many who have slipped beyond the mortal veil in very recent years. You will never be forgotten. Also, to my wife, for understanding. For everyone's help and encouragement, I am truly grateful.

CONTENTS

Contents

PREFACE

My lifelong love affair with the beautiful and historic Potomac River was the inspiration for this work, *Haunted Potomac River Valley*. Born near the river's mouth, I cut my eye teeth on the oysters and hard-shelled crabs pulled from its waters. During my earliest school years, I was amazed at how much of our nation's history entwined around the towns and valleys I knew and loved.

Over the years (and many weekend camping adventures), I discovered the many creeks and smaller rivers that fed the Potomac. I reveled in the mountains and the stories of the people who lived there. There isn't much of the river's waters my paddle hasn't been wet in.

My other love has always been scary tales and horror movies—especially those based on fact. It seemed natural to combine these two passions into a cohesive story of the river and its residents—living and dead. Do you believe in ghosts? According to a 2013 Huffington poll, 45 percent of adults do, and nearly a third of survey respondents claimed that they'd actually seen a specter. For myself, I've seen things I cannot explain. I've witnessed so-called shadow figures at the periphery of my vision in some of these places (concerning enough for me to see an optometrist). Do you believe? Are you like many who've felt death's icy-fingered caress from beyond the grave when no mortal being is there?

It is beyond the scope of this work to provide a full history of all the towns and locales mentioned here. In fact, the vast number of reported sightings and haunts along this river would require an encyclopedia-sized volume, but you will find the most notable and tragic tales described here in some detail. Did these innumerable tragedies give rise to restless spirits with unfinished business or one too enamored of the river to leave? In the end, I'll leave that for you to decide.

Acknowledgements

I'd like to acknowledge the many contributors to this book: Belinda Sue Kiser, a researcher and resident historian from Green Spring, West Virginia, and former Grant County, West Virginia magistrate Larry W. Ours. Janet Hughes of Shepherdstown Mystery Walks went above and beyond with tales from her town's history and her insights into its otherworldly inhabitants. 3 Notch Paranormal Investigations provided paranormal fodder through interviews and their YouTube video series *Haunted Southern Maryland*. Park maintenance program supervisor Greg Knott also contributed his sights and experiences. Special thanks also to Jayne C. Walsh (of Saint Clement's Island and Piney Point Lighthouse Museums) for providing the impetus for this effort and directing me to well-informed sources.

I'm also indebted to the storytellers at dozens of campfires throughout the years. Many of the fireside orators from my youth are gone, but they're not forgotten. Their faces in the firelight and the stories they told live on. Their shared tales and experiences were invaluable (and more than a bit scary). Their insights and shared memories involved many of the included locales and personalities, and their honesty, generosity and trust are cherished. Many others contributed their accounts but wanted to remain anonymous. I've respected their wishes, but their input is equally appreciated. I'm grateful to my exceptional editor Hayley Behal for her excellent insights and efforts. Last but not least, my appreciation goes to The History Press for these intriguing glimpses of history in an entertaining format. The Haunted America series literally brings the past alive.

INTRODUCTION

Paranormal activity has long been associated with waterways. It's been speculated that spiritual energies use water as a travel conduit, just as they do with electrical devices. The assertion is that water and electricity provide a spectral highway for travel between the worlds both seen and unseen. Judging from the volumes of associated reports, it is easy to surmise they are also a mode of communication from this alternate world. Apparently, the spirits find it easier to use these mediums to show us they are around or to get our attention. We see this referenced often in paranormal circles: lights blinking on and off, televisions cutting on by themselves and, of course, EVP (electronic voice phenomena). We hear of haunted waterfront houses and towns. There's so many tales of ghost ships and empty lighthouses (although deserted, still very active).

Of course, it takes more than water and a jolt of current to create a spectral being or a haunting (apologies to Mary Shelley). From my research and the numerous stories related to me, most authorities concede there is a trigger that keep the dearly departed from, well, departing. The consensus is that some unfinished business exists that the spirit feels compelled to complete, or a tragedy befell them at the end of their mortal lives. Some speculate that the love the deceased had for their home and lands might hold them here.

With this is mind, it stands to reason that a waterway most associated with paranormal activity would also be a historic one. The Potomac River certainly fits that category as one of the most historically significant waterways in the United States. (The name Potomac is derived from an Algonquian word meaning "a place to trade." An eighteenth-century spelling was *Patawomeke*.) The river flows over three hundred miles from the confluence of the North and South Branches to the Chesapeake Bay (four hundred miles from the source to the bay). Its ties to our history have earned it the nickname the "Nation's River."

The river's been used for centuries as a travel route (for mortals), and its waters have provided succulent bounty. People have occupied the region since 10,000 BC. Crabs, oysters, clams and a multitude of fish have graced the tables of those fortunate enough to live near its mouth. Upriver, the fish are also plentiful, as are the deer and turkey. Our forefathers from the headwaters at the Fairfax Stone to the river's mouth at the Chesapeake Bay in southern Maryland felt blessed to call the Potomac River valley their home.

The river's beauty is unquestioned. It's been a source of both the necessities of life and entertainment for generations. But many tragedies took root along its banks as well. Native Americans fought many battles here, only to be supplanted by a new people. The river formed a north/south boundary between the original colony states—a boundary that defined the front lines in the deadliest war in our history. The Civil War here truly turned brother against brother.

Pirates have plied their bloody trade here. Local wars were fought—over oysters! Riparian rights and ownership of the river has been the subject of Supreme Court cases. Four thousand souls perished from mistreatment at the U.S. POW camp at the river's mouth. Drownings, shipwrecks and floods have plagued the valley, as well as other more "normal" everyday tragedies.

With this background, is it any wonder that the valley contains several of the most haunted sites in the states that it flows through? Join me in my journey through the places and with the people along the historic and haunted Potomac River.

PART I

THE TWO HEADWATERS

THE TWO HEADWATERS, OR sources, of the Potomac pass through some of the most beautiful country in both Virginia and West Virginia. In some sections, they drain pastoral lands with rolling hills and epic views as far as the eye can see. In others, the tributaries twist and turn through rock-laden courses where rapids abound and eagles soar.

Politically, the Fairfax Stone in Eglon, West Virginia, is listed as the source of the Potomac—a convention that has been debated since the founding of Maryland and Virginia as royal colonies. A survey was conducted at the behest of Lord Fairfax by four Virginia surveyors: Colonel Peter Jefferson (Thomas Jefferson's father), Robert Brooke, Benjamin Winslow and Thomas Lewis. They placed the original Fairfax Stone in 1746.

From this marker, the North Branch flows west but soon twists north before settling into a southeastward course toward the Chesapeake Bay. The border between the two states remained an issue until 1910, when the Supreme Court ruled for Virginia. The decision was that Maryland would only go westward up the Potomac far enough to meet a point where a line drawn due north from the Fairfax Stone would cross that branch of the Potomac.

1
THE NORTH BRANCH TO THE CONFLUENCE

As the North Branch holds the honorarium as the Potomac's source, it seems appropriate to begin here. The North Branch travels ninety-seven miles from the Fairfax Stone to its confluence with the South Branch at Greenspring, West Virginia. A water journey on the North Branch is a more tumultuous ride than on the placid South Branch, although a dam at Jennings-Randolph Lake (in Garrett County, Maryland, and Mineral County, West Virginia) was built to minimize the flood damage of past years.

CUMBERLAND, MARYLAND

The first stop on our haunted journey is Cumberland, Maryland, on the North Branch of the Potomac. Several buildings in the area boast of a spectral presence in this old and historic town. Cumberland was established in 1787 by Europeans after centuries as a Native American village. It now boasts a thriving population of twenty thousand yet maintains a quaint small-town ambiance. It's known for its arts, but darker things also await a brave traveler.

Puccini Restaurant

Puccini Restaurant is a renovated two-hundred-year-old building. During the Civil War, it temporarily housed the wounded from that bloody period of our history. Guests and employees alike have reported "odd" sounds—like chairs being dragged across the floor. Footsteps in deserted areas of the building are also reported. These noises abruptly stop when investigated (for those brave enough to do so). Others noted they experienced no actual phenomena but simply felt watched.

A paranormal group, City Lights Paranormal Society from Easton, Pennsylvania, conducted an investigation into the supposed happenings using state-of-the-art electronic equipment. Their conclusion? Puccini is haunted.

Many sounds were collected on tape. There was a softly spoken "yes" to an unasked question. A child whimpered and a male voice seemed to say, "Raise your cup," when the group asked if any spirits were present. I imagine the hairs on everyone's necks also raised.

I plan a trip to Puccini soon to try its renowned pizza and to experience the possibly haunted atmosphere. Puccini Restaurant is famous for its wood-fired pizza and its hometown friendliness. If you are hesitant to share a meal with a possible ghost, perhaps you'd consider a literary sojourn with a spirit or two at our next stop?

Alleghany Library

The main Allegany County Library is located on Washington Street in Cumberland, and unexplained occurrences are the norm there. As is often the case with haunted buildings, the library is no stranger to tragic history. It is housed in a 170-year-old structure that was once a private academy and later a Civil War hospital. With that background, one can imagine the tragedies it's seen.

The basement area is the primary site of reported paranormal activity. It has been the focus of several paranormal investigations. A custodian reported tools and hardware being tossed about. Others have reported noises, such as the dragging of something heavy across the concrete floor. Some report a tug of their hair when there's no physical presence to account for it. Many stated their general feeling of unease or of a heaviness as they pass through certain areas in the library. Is it haunted? The investigators found evidence of it using their electronic measuring devices.

Local oral tradition holds that a Union soldier by the name of Francis Gillespie killed his commanding officer during the Civil War. He was imprisoned in the basement until such time as a military tribunal could try his case. He was found guilty and hanged. Legend claims that he appeared to a priest at St. Patrick's Church nearby to say his confession and plead forgiveness. Does Gillespie now haunt his old prison? Did the ghosts of the dead from the Civil War hospital never find peace?

Spring Gap Campground

Spring Gap Campground is located near Oldtown, Maryland, between Cumberland, Maryland, and Green Spring, West Virginia. It is situated on the North Branch of the Potomac bridging the two states along the Chesapeake and Ohio canal towpath. Its giant sycamore trees and oaks provide abundant shade, and wildflowers flourish here in the spring. Some visitors are attracted here not for the natural beauty but for its supernatural possibilities. Some haunted encounters and unexplained events have been reported here over the years. Most of the eyewitnesses report very similar experiences.

After enjoying a day of fishing and hiking at this popular campsite, the intrepid campers decide to retire to their tents set up near the river. At first, their slumbers are restful with only the sounds of the crickets, spring peepers and an occasional whippoorwill to lull them into an even deeper sleep. But all too soon, their sleep is interrupted by some unnamed souls—spirits not of this world.

Noises that are out of place in this rural setting stir them from their slumbers. There is the sound of voices, distant at first, but seeming to move toward the camp—closer and closer. Listening intently, with nerves on edge, the campers hear odd laughter just outside the thin nylon fabric of their tent.

Some campers say they hear their cooking utensils being moved about or the embers of their fire stirred or kicked out. A hungry raccoon perhaps? Or is it something more sinister that awaits the unsuspecting in the dark? Does a Shawnee brave of Indian Old Town (as Old Town was called after the Natives abandoned it) return to see what became of his former home? Or does frontiersman Thomas Cresap, out of his time, look for the trading post he established here in 1741?

One brave camper claims he gathered his courage and peeked through the tent opening when the voices drew close and saw two large men dressed in old-time clothing. When the two men noticed him looking, they disappeared. No smoke or fog marked their departure. No trees stirred to track their passage. No footprints remained at morning's light. One moment they were there and the next they were gone. He rubbed his eyes and wondered if he'd hallucinated, though others have reported similar experiences.

Green Spring, West Virginia

Green Spring, West Virginia, is a small town—a very small town, but it hasn't always been so. From its heyday as a railroad town and depot, it's become a small blip on the map, but its history and prominence are not forgotten by its residents. Geographically, it is an important location for any discussion of the Potomac's origins. On the map, the town marks the confluence of the North and South Branches that join to forge the mighty Potomac just east of its borders. The views around the town and this section of the river are of fertile valleys and mountain vistas.

Census records list a population of only 163 people residing in Green Spring. The town is the home of the House of the Setting Sun and Haunted Barn, an All Hallows' Eve attraction that runs for approximately one month annually. It is put on for charity and is one of the best such attractions I've visited. Every year, there's a different theme, and given the history of the town, one might wonder if some of the costumed actors aren't really acting at all.

The locally renowned Indian Rocks is another local attraction. The origin of the name is lost to history but not to legend. According to local historian Belinda Sue Kiser, folklore holds that a Native American man was killed and tied to the largest rock (now nearest the county road). Why? Well, one version says that his corpse was to serve as a warning to those of his people conducting raids on the sparsely populated white settlement. The other version states that the Native man fell in love with a white woman. Apparently, the lady in question shared his interest, and the man was killed for it. There's nothing in the oral tradition about what, if any, penalty was bestowed on the woman.

Many other events might have instigated the paranormal reports in the area. It has seen its fair share of spilled blood through vicious battles

Indian Rocks, Hampshire County, West Virginia. *From author's collection.*

during the Revolutionary War and Indian Wars continuing through the Civil War. Each left its own scar on the land and the people. Add in the nightmarish accidents associated with the railroad, the floods and outbreaks of deadly diseases, and many residents are left with an apathetic attitude toward death.

Hobos were a regular fixture even into the twentieth century, and many met their maker here. When a hobo was killed, it was common practice to cover the body with dirt right where they died, often within feet of the track. There was no proper burial, no family notification and no mourners—just raised mounds along the rails where body parts were covered with dirt to keep down the smell and deter scavengers.

During the Civil War, the Green Spring Depot was a major stop for wounded soldiers traveling north for aid. Many died right in town, long before ever reaching such care. Coffins came through as well, en route to their posthumous reunion with their loving families back home.

As one resident confided, "With all of this, we were bound to have some supernatural events. Things happen all the time that you can't explain. I grew up with the admonition to 'just ignore it,' like a little dirty secret.

People would dismiss events like it was perfectly normal to see a ghost walk by you while you watch TV."

Others, too, have experienced unexplainable noises from the woods and screams on the train tracks at night. Some have reported visions of ghostly apparitions walking the fields, along the tracks and down the back roads.

I'm told there are many homes in the area with ghostly house guests. The resident mentioned above said her aunt's home had a room that always stayed cold, no matter how hot the rest of the house was. In other houses, things went missing and doors opened and closed on their own. This is so common here that people rarely speak of it. If a ghost didn't do any real damage, then folks learned to live harmoniously with them. They make no explanations for the weird phenomena—it's just an accepted part of living in the area.

2
The South Branch to the Confluence

The South Branch of the Potomac begins in Highland County, Virginia, and travels two hundred miles to its confluence with the North Branch to form the main body of the Potomac River at Greenspring, West Virginia. From this confluence to the river's mouth at Point Lookout, Maryland, is another 302 miles. The South Branch is undammed throughout its length. This has added to the wildness and pristine nature of the river, although many floods have plagued the valley through the years.

Seneca Rocks, West Virginia

Seneca Rocks, West Virginia, is a popular stopping point for lovers of the local mountains. It's a scenic destination near the confluence of Seneca Creek and the North Branch. This area is beautiful and a grand spot for families to visit, but beware! Its darkness is both physical and supernatural. If you attempt the climb to the North Peak, you will encounter a warning sign that states fifteen people have died in falls there since 1971.

One of the prevailing legends of Seneca Rocks predates European settlement in the area. The oral tradition holds that Princess Snow Bird finally found a worthy suitor, her true love. As the only daughter of Chief Bald Eagle and his wife, White Rock, she had many braves vying for her hand. The rivalry between the braves became intense, and the chief decreed that it was time for her to choose. The method to use to pick her prospective mate was left to the young maiden. Snow Bird always loved gazing at the high peaks of the rocks and was among the few who'd ever dared to scale their heights. So, she made her decision.

Snow Bird summoned the eligible bachelors from throughout the area to meet at the base of Seneca Rocks. When they gathered, thinking her decision was made and each hoping to hear themselves named her mate, the princess instead announced that the first man to crest the peaks would be her betrothed. Being surefooted and familiar with the terrain, she personally led the way.

Most of the young men dropped out immediately, but seven braves fell in behind her in a race to the summit. Three dropped out at the first turn, gasping for breath. A fourth man slipped on loose stone and fell to his death. His scream echoed in the valley and was cut short when he met the rocks below.

Halfway up the rocks, a fifth man stumbled but caught himself. He dangled from a ledge, holding on for dear life. He dug his fingers into the rock, but his fingers began to slip—a hair's breadth at a time. When this man's grip failed, his scream did not abate. His body was mortally broken, but not immediately so.

Three quarters of the way to the summit, Snow Bird stopped to evaluate the contestants following her. She saw in the far distance as the sixth brave stopped, wiped his brow and turned back on the trail, defeated. As she paused, the seventh brave appeared in the twist in the trail and almost ran over her. In his haste to stop, he too slid from the narrow trail but caught a thin root to save himself. As the root began to break free, Snow Bird recognized him as the bravest and strongest of her people and pulled him to safety. They continued to the top together, hand in hand. The brave's worthy feat that day made him the successor to the king and earned the heart of the princess.

Is this what has caused the unrest among the spirits around this famous rock formation? Can the feeling of being watched, reported by so many, be attributed to them? Do the spirits of those fallen and defeated braves still lament their failures that day? Is it their footsteps that are heard walking the floors in the area when no mortal beings are stirring? Or is the cause of these local disturbances more recent in origin?

Knowing the land surrounding the rocks was a gathering place for the Seneca for generations, I'm told the Smithsonian excavated the area, and the findings and artifacts were removed to one of their museums. Some say the paranormal activity in the surrounding area began after these excavations

The peaceful South Branch of the Potomac. *From author's collection.*

were completed. They suggest that those footsteps you hear following you down an empty corridor are not made by flesh-and-blood beings. The doors that fling open and closed of their own accord? Well, it's said that this land is cursed by the Native Americans who once called it home.

Pay Seneca a visit. Climb at your own peril and let me know if you, too, feel the presence of its former residents.

PETERSBURG, WEST VIRGINIA

Petersburg is a mountain town sprawling around picturesque peaks and through fertile valleys. The town was founded in 1745 by Jacob Peterson. Mr. Peterson's claim to fame was ownership of the first mercantile store in the area.

Petersburg was one of the communities severely impacted by the flood of 1985. In the state, forty-seven people were killed in that flood. Pendleton and Grant Counties had the most fatalities. Towns such as Parsons, Rowlesburg,

Philippi, Marlinton, Glenville, Petersburg and Moorefield saw severe damage. The South Branch crested about ten feet above flood stage and nearly four feet higher than during the June 1949 flood, the previous record. The 1985 flood caused an estimated $570 million in damages. More than 3,500 homes and 180 businesses were destroyed.

But West Virginians are a hardworking and stoic people. They play the cards they're dealt and get on with the business of living. As I've found to be the case in most of the towns in the Mountain State, Petersburg is a friendly place—a town where you know most of your neighbors and a stranger is usually greeted with a smile and a warm welcome.

During the 2010 census, the population of Petersburg numbered just under twenty-five hundred souls, but census workers only count the living.

This story is not the result of any of the aforementioned floods. It's not one of the many reports of whispered voices while floating the river or feelings of unease as the site of a former homestead is passed by. I suspect it is a story of a reluctant spirit who loved her mountain home too much to leave—and it's a story I'm inclined to believe. It came to me from one of Grant County's finest, a longtime resident of Petersburg and a past member of the sheriff's office.

To the best of the then-deputy's memory, this occurred around 1982. A county resident called the sheriff's office with a request to meet up with a deputy, if one was in their area, so they'd not have to make the drive into town. For some unexplained reason, the caller did not want to meet at his own home. The nearest deputy was radioed with the request. He asked the dispatcher to relay the meeting place to the citizen. He chose a well-known landmark, an abandoned two-story white house along the South Branch.

When the deputy arrived, he found two men waiting at the end of the driveway. As there was no shoulder on the road, the officer recognized the unsafe situation and waved at the men to follow him. He pulled his squad car in close to the house.

"What are you doing, deputy?" they asked. "You're sure to wake the lady up."

"What lady? No one's lived here in half a dozen years. Not since the old widow woman passed on. It was cancer I think," the deputy answered.

"No sir, officer. That's why we were wondering why you picked this spot. We were out this way last week about dusk, thinking the place was deserted, and an elderly lady was sitting at the window, gazing out over the mountain and brushing her hair. It was long and white as cotton. We didn't want to scare the old lady, so we were waiting out at the end of the road for you."

"I'm telling you nobody lives here." The deputy swung his flashlight toward the house and switched it on to highlight the front windows, one by one. Each was broken with but few shards of glass remaining. "Which window are you thinking you saw this mystery woman at?"

He could see each man shake as if a chill ran down their backs. Both of them swore to the truth of their original sighting and to their sobriety on the night in question. Although the forlorn lady was not a victim of the 1985 flood, the old white homestead was. If the lady's spirit was still attached to her ancestral home as the waters rose to sweep her home away, I hope she found peace.

Romney, West Virginia

Romney is a small suburban town and the county seat of Hampshire County, West Virginia. It shares the title of the oldest town in West Virginia with Shepherdstown. Both were established by the Virginia House of Burgesses and approved by the governor on December 23, 1762.

In the census of 2010, there were 1,848 people, 843 households and 410 families living in the city limits. Romney is an old town that's known its share of both joys and tragedies. Hunters and traders founded the town in 1725, when it was known as Pearsall's Flats. The name was later changed to Romney in deference to the port town of Romney, Kent, England, by Thomas Fairfax, Sixth Lord Fairfax of Cameron. The town honors its colonial roots with a variety of period place-names. The West Virginia Schools for the Deaf and Blind is located here.

Driving down the Northwestern Turnpike (also known as U.S. Route 50), one encounters the Indian Mound Cemetery. This Hopewellian mound overlooking the South Branch of the Potomac is known as the Romney Indian Mound. It's also the site of the nation's first Confederate memorial, the former Fort Pearsall, Parsons Bell Tower and reinterments from Romney's Old Presbyterian Cemetery. Indian Mound Cemetery is the burial site of two governors of West Virginia, a member of the United States House of Representative, a United States secretary of the army and a former owner of the Washington Redskins. Some of George Washington's descendants also reside here.

History plays a prominent role in this town and in the minds of its progeny. The most critical period for the town was during the War Between

Indian Mound Cemetery, Romney, West Virginia. *From author's collection.*

Left: Indian Mound Sign, Romney, West Virginia. *From author's collection.*

Below: Old Hampshire County jail, Romney, West Virginia. *From author's collection.*

the States. Romney paid a heavy price during those turbulent times. The town changed hands an estimated fifty-six times. Romney knew all too well the horror of conflicted families, of brother against brother, in this bloody time. One of many examples of this is seen at the Davis History House (circa 1798) on West Main Street. The Davis family sent two sons to fight for the Confederacy and one for the Union. It is now restored as a museum featuring Civil War artifacts and furnishings from that era.

Many residences were turned into emergency hospitals, such as the Boxwood residence (circa 1850) on East Main Street. It is said that all fifty-six changes between the Northern and Southern armies occurred in this home's front yard.

Many have reported strange happenings in the historic homes near Romney and along the South Branch, but the river itself provides an ominous history as well. Long ago, the Shawnee claimed that the banks of the South Branch River were haunted by evil spirits. Some say they are still here and are seen as shadowy spirits ghosting along the river's banks in the early morning light or in the hushed moments just before full dark.

Old Hampshire County Jail was built in the latter part of the 1700s, but the paranormal activity associated with it didn't begin until approximately a century later. That is when the local county sheriff was shot and killed by bandits determined to turn his town into their personal playground. The sheriff entered the top of the staircase leading from the sheriff's home to the jail, preparing to start his day. When he turned at the top step, the gang opened fire on him. The sheriff fell and tumbled down the stairs, mortally wounded. Witnesses to this day report hearing that sound in the dark of the night. The *thump*, *thump*, *thump* of the sheriff's corpse bouncing its way into the hereafter.

PART II

A River Is Born

Beginning at the confluence, the river now takes on its own identity. Before this point, its tributaries marked the outline of the watershed. These feeder streams and rivers are primarily named after the river they give birth to: North Fork South Branch of the Potomac, South Fork North Branch of the Potomac, et cetera. From here to the river's mouth, the river's tributaries own their names. The river also earns its name independent of North and South designations. From here to the river's mouth, it's simply the Potomac. Historic rivers such as the Shenandoah and the Cacapon add their waters to the Potomac as it continues its tireless race to the Chesapeake Bay.

3
Paw Paw, West Virginia

Paw Paw is a small town very near the confluence of the two sections of the Potomac—the North and South Branches in Morgan County, West Virginia. The population was listed at only 508 in the 2010 census. Paw Paw was incorporated on April 8, 1891, and named for the pawpaw, a native fruit that grows in abundance throughout the region.

The Paw Paw Tunnel is one of the landmarks the town is known for. The tunnel was completed in 1850 as part of the Chesapeake and Ohio Canal (C&O). Its creation was intended to serve as a bypass to the rough terrain around Paw Paw bends. Work was slow, arduous and hazardous—so much so that the contractors missed their proposed completion date by twelve years. Working with only hand tools and dynamite, progress was severely hampered, with an average advance of only twelve feet per day. That's little more than a scratch when you have 3,118 feet of solid rock to carve through. Cave-ins were not unusual during construction, and there were many work-related injuries and deaths. At one point, cholera swept through the workforce.

Many foreigners were brought in to construct the tunnel. They were predominantly immigrant workers from Germany, Ireland and England. The workers were paid a pauper's wages (assuming they were paid at all given the frequent financial difficulties facing the companies that employed them). The working conditions were horrendous by modern standards. Far from home with low pay and poor living conditions, it was only a matter of time before tensions among the diverse group exploded and bloody riots engulfed the work camps.

The brawls led to the destruction of local saloons and other notable establishments. The lockhouse at lock 64 2/3 burned down overnight, and the slain body of the lockkeeper was found inside. His murderer was never found.

The violence associated with the tunnel continued well after the sound of the last stone hammer and chisel rang across the Potomac. The tunnel was designed to accommodate the passage of one boat at a time. However, the boat captains, whether ignorant of the rules or intolerant of them, ignored the right-of-way rules on a regular basis, resulting in many bloody confrontations.

Many have reported feeling watched as they've traversed the tunnel. Some have seen ghostly shadow figures flitting about just at the edge of the darkest portions of the tunnel. Is it the ghost of the lockkeeper still making his appointed rounds or in search of his murderer? Or one of many who perished building the tunnel? Paranormal specialists have described seeing these shadows as well as recording disembodied whispers from the beyond.

The history of violence in this dark, dank tunnel might explain the many reports of haunted activity here. If you ever get a chance to visit the tunnel, you'll see the thinnest beam of light at the opposite end. Add the cold and wet atmosphere and it's scary enough—even if you aren't treated to a spectral visit. Take the walk through if you're brave. Goosebumps are all but guaranteed.

4

Great Cacapon, West Virginia

Great Cacapon is a small town in Morgan County, West Virginia, situated near the confluence of the Cacapon River with the Potomac. The Cacapon's name is derived from a Native American word meaning "the medicine waters." As of the 2010 census, its population was 386. The following is excerpted from a story told to me by a former resident.

In 1985, she was a young mother with a nine-year-old son. She rented a two-story round stone cabin that was said to be former slave quarters. It sat in a beautiful location near the river and far enough from the main colonial-era farmhouse to provide privacy. Thick woods surrounded the back of the home. Additions were made to the original structure over the years, but the stone portion was said to be over 150 years old. Not much else was known about the history of the building.

Despite the welcoming atmosphere she felt on the grounds during the day, at night, the cabin took on a whole different ambiance. The lights seldom worked properly at night. The electric was fine during the day, but at night, they would flicker and stay out until morning. She asked the owner about possible shorts in the wiring, but his response was that the wiring was old but perfectly safe.

His half-hearted explanations frustrated her, but not wanting to make a fuss, she adjusted to evening candlelight.

Her son's bedtime on school nights was 8:00 p.m. The living room was upstairs adjacent to his bedroom, while her bedroom and the kitchen were on the first floor. She fell into the habit of reading in her room after her son went to bed. She'd watch TV on the rare occasions they had power. That's when things got weirder.

For a period of some months and multiple times each week, she'd hear a very soft female voice singing what sounded like a lullaby. It was coming from upstairs where her son should be sleeping.

The first few times this occurred, the power happened to be on. She concluded that her son had snuck out of his room and turned on the TV or was playing the radio. She hurried up the stairs, only to find him fast asleep. She then settled back in her own room, figuring it was only her imagination after all, when the singing started up again.

This continued for some time. She was often kept awake all hours listening to the haunting melody of the unseen singer; she could never make out the words, but the music sent chills up her spine. One morning when she was thoroughly frustrated from lack of sleep, she broached the subject with her son.

"Did you hear all the singing last night?" she asked.

"Yeah, Mom, I hear it all the time." He shrugged and, with no change in his demeanor, continued to eat his breakfast. It was as if he'd been asked about the weather.

"So, you can hear the singing at night?"

"Yeah mom, what's up? It's just an old Black lady. She's the ghost that lives here. She sings to her baby at night. Don't worry, she won't hurt you."

"This doesn't bother you?" she asked, trying to sound nonchalant.

"No." He looked at her as a dead silence fell between them for several seconds. She felt as if he was challenging her feelings about the spirit.

"Does the singing keep you up?" she asked.

"It kinda…helps me sleep," he replied and, with that, headed out the door for school.

Later that evening, when they were eating dinner, the subject came up again. Her son said he'd first seen the spectral lady singer soon after they moved in. He said her singing was fine, but he didn't like the little boy who played with his toys and got him in trouble all the time.

After this conversation, her son convinced her that the ghosts meant no harm. She did ask the ghost not to sing so that she'd hear it. Her son might enjoy it, but she did not. After her request, she rarely heard it again. Strange things did continue, but they adapted to the activity.

The singing lady was the most dramatic happening experienced at the cabin but far from the only one. She stated that from her first night in the cabin, she unconsciously ignored a lot of things that didn't appear quite "normal." In the woods behind the cabin, she often felt she was watched and on occasion saw red glowing eyes in the distance watching. Her woodland walks stopped after that. Many times, objects were moved around their home or disappeared altogether. In her youth, she was no stranger to such events, and she'd learned to say out loud, "Whoever took my things, please return them, thank you." Sure enough, the item would soon reappear. She said this worked with the spirits at the cabin, as well as with those she experienced in her past.

They resided in the cabin for less than a year when the 1985 flood washed them out. Although she'd learned to coexist with the otherworldly roommates and lost her fear of them, she says it's been many years since she's experienced anything more disturbing than the eerie late-night lullabies.

5

SHEPHERDSTOWN, WEST VIRGINIA

Shepherdstown is touted as the most haunted town in West Virginia. It also shares the title of the oldest town in the state (an honor it disputes with Romney, West Virginia—both established in 1762). Also, like Romney, Shepherdstown hosted some of the bloodiest battles of our Civil War period. Historically (and paranormally), it is known primarily for its Civil War period despite the fact that many graves here mark the passing of soldiers from the French and Indian War and the Revolutionary War. But the Battle of Antietam was fought only four miles away. Eight thousand of the twenty-three thousand wounded or killed were dumped on the small town to care for (or dispose of). A local saying about this period is that it was "one big field hospital, and the streets ran with blood." There is little wonder then that this period in the town's history is recalled so well.

A little-known fact is that Shepherdstown vied for acceptance as our nation's capital. It was George Washington's first choice for the seat of government, but fate conspired against the town. The river level was too low that year and would not readily allow water transportation. In addition, the bid was received too late for final consideration. Thus but for lack of rain and either bureaucratic sluggishness or postal delays, Shepherdstown might be the nation's capital today. But then, the town's peace and sweet ambiance would now be lost to the pages of history.

To classify Shepherdstown, one must embrace the paradox it represents. It is a peaceful, friendly town that manages to combine small-town ambiance with amenities usually reserved for much larger towns. It is both a historic

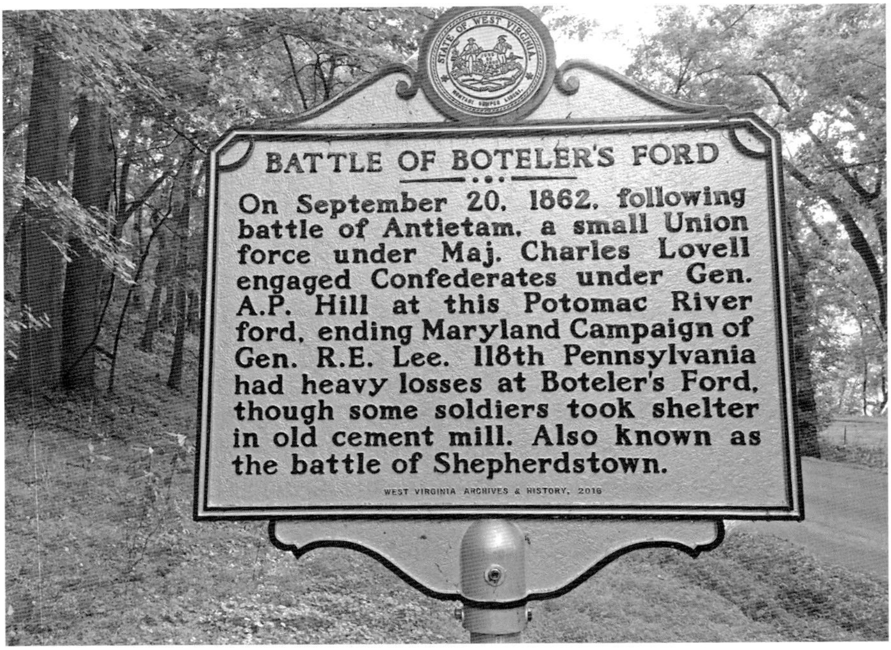

Above: Plaque at site of Battle of Shepherdstown, West Virginia. *From author's collection.*

Left: Shepherdstown tour guide Janet Hughes. *Courtesy Janet Hughes.*

and a forward-thinking town, a railroad town, a water town and a college town. It boasts a permanent residency of 2,000 residents, but the student population swells its streets with an additional 3,400 souls—assuming we count only the living and breathing inhabitants. The crime rate here is a mere 2 percent. On a recent visit, the mayor met us on our walkabout the town during a ghost tour. He stopped to say hello, introduced himself and inquired about our well-being. Other villagers we met added to the welcoming atmosphere of the town.

But Shepherdstown is as renowned for its apparitions as it is for the friendliness of its inhabitants. The "others" were the subject of a television show, *Ghosts of Shepherdstown*, that aired for two seasons, 2016–17. After due diligence in researching the town, the extraordinary number of reports and evidence found here—anecdotal and otherwise—led us to one of the premier ghost tours in the region. Janet Hughes of Shepherdstown Mystery Walks provided much of the history and the stories provided here.

Shepherdstown Sweet Shop + Bakery

Shepherdstown Sweet Shop & Bakery is well known for its tasty pastries, as well as its gory past. The building was one of several commandeered for use as a hospital after the bloody Battle of Antietam. This particular field hospital was focused on amputations during the Confederate occupation after the Battle of Antietam (as well as the Battle of Shepherdstown the following day). Historical records describe the second floor in a manner reminiscent of an assembly line, with cutting, sawing, cauterizing and bandaging occurring on virtually every flat surface. Piles of severed hands and feet decorated one corner and bloody remnants of soldiers' arms and legs in another. Wagons pulled up outside of a second-story window, and the miscellaneous body parts were tossed into the grisly flatbed carts like so much cordwood, then to be dumped into the nearby Potomac. (Bones were discovered during a recent renovation of the street below, and the Smithsonian has expressed interest in doing an archeological dig there.)

The establishment might have an otherworldly patron—a special guest who's been dubbed "The Colonel." Some have said they've felt his presence brush past them and have overheard the murmured conversations of invisible entities while enjoying their sweet treats.

Shepherdstown Sweet Shop Bakery. *From author's collection.*

STONE ROW ON NEW STREET

Stone Row on New Street has a reputation as being the site of several hauntings. The first level of the building is made of limestone rock and was built in 1792 by Hessian soldiers. It was initially used as a brewery. The upper level was added in the early 1800s to house the Irish laboring on the nearby C&O canal. The Irish were considered second-class citizens (at best) and faced atrocious living conditions there. It was severely crowded, and over three hundred died when a tuberculosis outbreak ravaged the town. The attitude was to replace those deceased with fresh Irishmen as soon as possible—the canal building must go on.

The building was converted into townhouses, and after the horrors of the Civil War passed, the forgotten non-combatants were also left to carry on. One was a mother named Rachel Snyder. A recent widow, she found herself in dire straits economically. Nearly destitute, she found a cheap rental space here in what was then the bad side of town. It wasn't long after taking up residence with her children that odd occurrences began to happen. After

Stone Row, Shepherdstown, West Virginia. *From author's collection.*

she and the children retired to their rooms at night, they'd hear footsteps moving down the stairs and often mischievous laughter as if from a child. Doorknobs were seen twisting slowly open. On occasion, they heard a sound they described as the swishing of a long dress and then a baby crying as footsteps descended the stairs. The crying would cease then as if muffled by a not-so-human hand.

A priest blessed the building, and the hauntings stopped—for a while. There are still reports of the sounds of a baby crying. People on the tour of this street have seen a woman staring at them from the shadows and from behind ornamental bushes. They felt she was imploring them for help. Could it be that Rachel Snyder has returned to seek aid from the living? Does she still fear for her little ones' safety?

Shepherd Family Cemetery

Shepherd Family Cemetery is the gated final resting place of the founder's family, interred from 1776 to 1941. Unusual for a family burial plot—especially in that time period—the household's enslaved people were buried among the plots of the family.

This is where Cecil the cat, the unofficial "mascat" of the tour, joined us for a brief respite. The feline appeared to be of the flesh and blood variety and exhibited no otherworldly attributes (at least no more so than any other cat). Other apparitions, however, have been seen here. These include the vision of the bottom half of Union soldiers walking on the street outside. The blue pants and yellow stripes were easily discernable, but where their upper bodies should be, there was only air. Could this be two men who gave their lives in defense of their country's union, only to meet with Confederate cannon fire?

Several young children, when visiting this site, have asked if they could go play with the "other children" in the graveyard—children, by the way, that no one else could see. One must wonder what any parent's response to that query might be.

This is also the graveyard where a "man" has been photographed floating near the rock wall surrounding the graveyard. Some state that he seems to be levitating, while others are convinced that he is astride a horse. As he is seen only from the waist up, this question might never be answered.

Shepherd Family Cemetery, Shepherdstown, West Virginia. *From author's collection.*

Trinity House

Trinity House is adjacent to the burial plot and the rectory for Trinity Episcopal Church and is the next foray into the historic and unexplained. During the Battle of Antietam, many fled the inevitable collision of the two mighty armies. Reverend Charles Andrews and his wife, Sarah remained. True Christians in belief and action, they were renowned for their generosity and hospitality to all needy souls. On the fatal day, as bodies piled up in the town, Sarah wrote a letter to her daughter detailing the carnage. She described the bodies littering the streets to the point that ambulances could not pass. She said the floors of Trinity House were covered with the bodies of the sick and dying and that it was the same throughout the small town. Due to the benevolence of the long-deceased couple, our tour guide surmised that it is none other than Charles Andrews who's seen floating in the graveyard, ensuring that all is as it should be in his town and parish.

Haunted window at Trinity House, Shepherdstown, West Virginia. *From author's collection.*

Trinity Episcopal Church

Trinity Episcopal Church was built in 1859 and its nearby chapel in 1870. Prior to the church's erection, the site was the field where local militia practiced military drills. This continued through the French and Indian War up until just before the Civil War. There were thirteen churches in town at that time. When bodies were piled high in every building in town, the local pastors pleaded with the Confederates holding the town. This was a devout town, and townspeople felt their churches were being desecrated with the dying soldiers and the rotting corpses of the dead. The Confederates agreed to allow Trinity Church to remain "unbloodied" as a field hospital, as it was the newest of the town's churches.

It was some years later before the fruits of human suffering created the breeding ground for a haunting here. In the 1940s, Serena Dandridge taught Sunday school at the church chapel. The townspeople nicknamed her "Miss

Trinity Church, Shepherdstown, West Virginia. *From author's collection.*

Violet." She was a talented artist and poet but was also described in those days as "touched." She was often seen arguing on the street with people nobody else could see, and her mental issues were well known throughout the town. Her illness seemed benign, however, and she was a devout woman. Her students all loved her, so with a watchful eye from the community, she continued teaching.

All went well until the well-known grove of cedars near town developed a blight. It was not a terminal condition but an unsightly one as the trees became nearly barren of needles. Apple orchards were a big cash crop in the area, and the town fathers feared the blight might next attack the fruit of their labors. The decision was made—the trees must go.

Serena pleaded with them to change their minds. She loved the giant ancient trees and could not imagine her town stripped of their glory. She wrote letters and staged protests—even if she was the only one in attendance. She cornered anyone who'd listen to beseech their support, but it was all to no avail.

On the night before the trees were due to be destroyed, Serena fled her home for the sanctuary of her trees. She placed hundreds of American flags around the base of the cedars and chained herself to two of them. When the workers arrived, she begged them to not destroy her friends. The police were called, and Ms. Dandridge was arrested and sent to Sheppard Pratt Mental Hospital in Baltimore. Conventional wisdom decrees that she died there some years later, but that's not the story many local folks believe. The rumor in town is that Serena took her own life. It's said that she hanged herself in, or just outside of, the chapel she loved. It's also believed by many that she never left. Many have seen a spectral woman by the tree outside of the chapel. Photographs have been taken of a woman peering through the window of the chapel when no one is inside. There's a report of a blue ball that appears to be composed of static bouncing and then floating back inside. Did Serena Dandridge love her little chapel too much to abandon it to the living?

Bilmyer Corner

Bilmyer Corner in town is also called by another name—Poltergeist Corner. The origin of the name is unknown, but the reason for the local moniker is known by many. Groups of people have observed a dark male shadow sitting

Town Run, Shepherdstown, West Virginia. *From author's collection.*

on a stoop there who often stands, walks away and disappears—even as they watch. Other shadowy figures have also been attested to. A teashop once operated on the corner. The owner was a believer and knew the reputation of the shop, and her first order of business was to assure the "spirits" that they could cohabitate peacefully with no interference from her. They must

Abandoned blast furnace near site of Battle of Shepherdstown, West Virginia. *From author's collection.*

have believed her, as she operated successfully there for twenty years. When her retirement was imminent, she found a buyer for her shop. The new owner was also aware of the teashop's reputation and decided to exploit it. If mere rumors of a haunting drew in the customers, she'd offer seances and Ouija boards along with beverages and tasty treats. She knew that would really pull them in. The teashop closed after less than six months. Did the spirits feel disrespected? The lady didn't hang around long enough to ask.

Shepherdstown is not without its associations with the rich and famous. Many authors have at one time or another found inspiration here. Hollywood types have also made an appearance. In the 1990s, Mary Tyler Moore bought the home of one of her ancestors, a coppersmith by trade. She refurbished the building and donated it to the college for use as a museum. This same building served as a church office in 1895. That's when a clergyman hanged himself inside. It's said that this ethereal being is often seen sitting on the porch to this day, the smell of his tobacco smoke filling the air.

THE OLD ENGLISH CEMETERY

The Old English Cemetery is considered by investigators to be a very active site. It contains graves dating to the Revolutionary War through the French and Indian War and, of course, the Civil War period. Many of the graves have Old English engravings, and I assume they are the source of the name. Many are also unmarked—the stone engravings lost to the abrasions of time. It is owned by Trinity Church and was our next stop. The first impression of the graveyard was the smell of smoke where none could be seen. When we left and circled the area, no smoke could be seen. We're told this is a common occurrence for other visitors to the site.

Sightings of a woman and a young inhuman girl (perhaps past-human girl is more accurate) walking along the back wall are commonplace. Many speculate that this is a mother and daughter retracing steps they took in life or a tragic time repeated for eternity when a loved one was lost. But it's the back corner of the site that draws your eye as you enter. I'm told many feel a malevolent spirit when passing through the ancient stones there. Nausea, headaches and shortness of breath are the normal result for folks

Old English Cemetery, Shepherdstown, West Virginia. *From author's collection.*

considered to be sensitives. I confess to feeling a bit of intestinal unease myself when we returned to the site after the tour. Power of suggestion or a real experience? I cannot say.

As to the smell? Some believe it's the supernatural remnants of past funeral processions and the many lit torches and lanterns accompanying them. Others state the smell is more earthy, the scent of horse manure to be exact, remembered echoes from the same source—the final journey for the guest of honor's pageant.

Beside the cemetery is the Mecklenburg Chapel, built in 1734 of log construction. It burned down in 1768 and was immediately rebuilt in fireproof stone. Its foundation is original and has been in continuous use since its creation. It was converted to apartments for collegians and recently served as the headquarters for the paranormal television show about Shepherdstown.

Shepherd University

Shepherd University was founded in 1871, and a boiler explosion razed the first school building (now known as Knutti Hall) five years later. No one perished in the explosion; however, students still report the smell of smoke in the rooms of the rebuilt structure. Terrified screams are reported. Rumors abound of a woman running the halls with half of her face burned off, only to disappear. As there were no fatalities, one must assume death is not a prerequisite to a haunting. It appears that extreme human pain and horror alone can also breed these reflected memories of the past.

McMurran Hall

McMurran Hall was one of the many hospitals located here during the Civil War. Once serving as the town hall, it was commissioned by Rezen Shepherd (son of founder Thomas Shepherd) in 1858 on their original homesite. Rezen gifted the building to the town. In time, the town gifted the building to the university and now operates as the administration building.

During the Civil War, the clock tower was in the process of being moved from the church tower to this building—the new town hall. Scaffolding

Clock Tower Shepherdstown University Building. *From author's collection.*

was erected many stories high as the tower building progressed. It was near completion when Antietam happened. When the eight thousand sick and wounded arrived in Shepherdstown and there was no more space to "store" the sick and deceased, a brilliant idea was put forth: "Let's stack 'em on the scaffolding." Straw was laid down across the boards, and bodies piled on the scaffolding that seemed to reach to the clouds. It surely appeared as if mankind made a second attempt to scale the heavens, this time offering up its own dead and nearly dead as an offering.

These horrors still reverberate today. Students report strange noises and other apparitions here. More alarming, if you're strolling the grounds late at night, look up at the clock tower. There you might be one of the "lucky" ones to see a shadowy figure or disembodied head observing you from above. Is it the ghost of Thomas Shepherd watching over his town, the town that bears his name? Or is it one of the Civil War soldiers left there to die?

The Entler-Weltzheimer House

The Entler-Weltzheimer House, also known as the "Little Yellow House," is located on the north side of High Street. It was once the site of a fort during the French and Indian War, and its construction is dated somewhere between 1770 and 1793. The original structure was of logs that have since been covered with a modern wood siding.

The peaceful Potomac at the site of the Battle of Shepherdstown. *From author's collection.*

The source of the haunting is from many years later, when the owner, a cobbler by the name of George Yontz, was found murdered outside his home in 1910. I've found no evidence that his murderer was ever brought to justice.

Local tradition has it that his ghost still haunts the building that's now in use by Shepherd College. Some claim the house and grounds are cursed. Others report the tapping of the cobbler's tools in the dead of the night. Is George still seeking his justice? Or revenge on the living?

Many more tales exist in this small town, many undocumented or not repeated for fear of the impression such a story might evoke. Shortly after our arrival, our excellent guide stated, "This town is very good to its dead." It's good to its residents and visitors as well. When it comes to Shepherdstown, West Virginia, whether you are a believer or not, or even if you hide under the bed at any sound that goes bump in the night, a visit here is highly recommended.

6

Antietam Sharpsburg, Maryland

The small towns of Antietam and Sharpsburg are best known for their tragic historic significance. The Battle of Antietam holds the dubious distinction of being the bloodiest battle ever fought on American soil. Approximately twenty-three thousand men were killed, wounded or listed as missing.

On the heels of a series of victories in the summer of 1862, including the decisive Second Battle of Manassas, General Robert E. Lee penned a letter to Confederate president Jefferson Davis. He wrote, "The present seems to be the most propitious time since the commencement of the war for the Confederate Army to enter Maryland."

The Maryland Campaign began on September 4. Luck was not on Lee's side, however, as a copy of Lee's Special Order 191, outlining his battle plan, was discovered. It was quickly relayed to Union general McClellan. On receipt of this intel, McClellan made very clear his respect for the Confederate general. History reports that he stated, "Now I know what to do….Here is a paper with which, if I cannot whip Bobby Lee, I will be willing to go home."

On September 17, 1862, the first hostilities broke out near Dunker Church and in nearby Miller's Cornfield. The battle lasted for about twelve hours. The Union's Army of the Potomac attacked the Confederate's left flank, but Confederate general Stonewall Jackson's army held the line.

Some of the heaviest fighting began at the Sunken Road, also known today as Bloody Lane. Confederates were entrenched along the depression in the aptly named road. The battle here lasted for nearly four hours.

Mumma Cemetery, Antietam, Maryland. *From author's collection.*

The third and final engagement of the battle was at a stone bridge now known as Burnside Bridge. Five hundred Georgians from Lee's army held off approximately fourteen thousand Union soldiers for several hours. Eventually, Union general Ambrose Burnside was able to rally his troops and, with their far superior numbers, captured the bridge to advance toward the Confederate's right flank.

The Battle of Antietam (also known as the Battle of Sharpsburg) ended when Confederate reinforcements arrived on the scene. Historians count the battle as a draw, but many consider it to be the turning point of the war. The Confederacy did not gain this needed victory and its desired foothold in the North—something potential European allies were waiting for. The Confederates were forced to retreat back into Virginia.

Antietam is currently (as of the 2010 census) listed as having a population of eighty-nine. Sharpsburg proper boasted over seven hundred inhabitants in the same census.

The historic Civil War National Park Battlefield at Antietam is said to be haunted by the ghosts of soldiers. Is it any wonder, given the mass casualties and horrors visited upon fellow Americans here? The sounds of phantom

Sunken Road, Antietam, Maryland. *From author's collection.*

Opposite, top: Dunkard Church, Antietam, Maryland. *From author's collection.*

Opposite, bottom: Burnside Bridge, Antietam, Maryland. *From author's collection*

Left: Frederick Douglas. *Library of Congress.*

Below: Puffenburger Farm, Antietam, Maryland. *From author's collection.*

gunfire and shouts are often heard, and drumbeats and war songs echo in the ears of those considered sensitive to the otherworldly sounds.

Visitors have reported seeing "ghost shadows" passing in front of their headlight beams as they exit the park. Figures of soldiers walking and running along the fence line is not uncommon. In fact, several witnesses have stopped to admire the realistic activities of reenactors—only to have them disappear before them.

Cornfield Cannons, Antietam, Maryland. *From author's collection.*

Another visitor claimed to have been approached by an elderly gent dressed in a Civil War–style uniform near the Burnside Bridge. As did other folks in a similar scenario, he assumed the man to be a reenactor who'd strayed from his group. The man walked toward him from the hillside and made a remark about the "horror of it all." When the agreeable tourist turned to reply, the man was gone. He still wonders if somehow his own imagination played a trick on him that day. After all, aren't sites stained with past horrors known to absorb the historic atmosphere? You don't have to be a "sensitive" to feel the heaviness in the air here. The aura is dark, and to this day, the suffering exudes from the very earth beneath your feet.

Is it possible that many so-called hauntings are the result of our imaginations tinged with knowledge of a place's horrid past? Or is it as one frequent visitor stated: "I have no doubt in my mind that the battlefield is haunted. Nothing else can explain what I've seen."

You can begin your visit (haunted or otherwise) at Antietam National Battlefield Visitor Center at 5831 Dunker Church Road, Sharpsburg, Maryland 21872.

PART III

MOUNTAINS TO THE PIEDMONT

THIS SECTION INCLUDES BOTH the geographical transition from mountains to foothills and the line between the free-flowing and tidal portions of the river. Little Falls marks this dividing line at the end of a ten-mile stretch of rapids, falls and swift-flowing water. It also marks the river's "head of navigation." Ships cannot navigate upstream from this point.

Confederates crossing the Potomac from period woodcut. *Harper's Weekly.*

7
Harpers Ferry, West Virginia

Harpers Ferry is a quiet, historic village in Jefferson County, West Virginia. It lies at the confluence of the Shenandoah and Potomac Rivers in the Blue Ridge Mountains where West Virginia, Virginia and Maryland converge. It is the lowest point in West Virginia. The town's population has dwindled from its heyday and was listed at less than three hundred residents during the 2010 census. It is the most eastern town in West Virginia and during the Civil War was the northernmost point of Confederate-controlled territory. The town's original, lower section was built on a floodplain created by the two rivers and surrounded by high ground. The frequent flooding occurring here over time also diminished the number of full-time residents.

Peter Stephens settled the area in 1732. At that time, history only remembers it as the place where the two rivers meet. In 1747, Robert Harper bought settlement rights from Stephens and operated a ferry to cross the Potomac River in 1761. On October 25, 1783, Thomas Jefferson visited Harpers Ferry and later documented his visit. In particular, he described the views from a rock ledge (now named Jefferson's Rock). He described it as "perhaps one of the most stupendous scenes in nature" and added, "This scene is worth a voyage across the Atlantic." High praise indeed, considering the ardors of an ocean voyage in colonial times.

The town has a long and rich history, but the period it is most known for (and which likely gave rise to most of the ghost tales told here) began

Above: Jefferson's Rock, Harper's Ferry, West Virginia. *From author's collection.*

Left: John Brown Monument, Antietam, Maryland. *From author's collection.*

The Point, the confluence of Shenandoah and Potomac Rivers, Harper's Ferry, West Virginia. *From author's collection.*

on Sunday, October 16, 1859. The town was part of Virginia at that time and was the site of John Brown's Raid, also known as the Harpers Ferry Raid. Historians consider this to be one of the major incidents fomenting the Civil War.

Brown chose Harpers Ferry because of the military arsenal harbored there. In addition, the town's location provided easy access to the South. His long-term strategy was to free the enslaved people via a grassroots rebellion, and Harpers Ferry was to be his starting point. One hundred thousand weapons were stored at the arsenal, and the encircling Blue Ridge Mountains provided an ideal spot for his planned guerrilla warfare. Brown attacked with a band of twenty-one men. This "army of liberation" was composed of sixteen white and five Black men (three were born as free Black men, one was a freed slave and one a fugitive slave). They seized the armory and other strategic points under cover of darkness on that fateful Sunday in October. The townsfolk and the nearby countryside were alerted to the attack, and a combined force of state and federal troops defeated the raiders (Brown's "army of liberation") in thirty-six hours. Seventeen men died, including two of Brown's own sons.

The raid was denounced by most of the country. Southern slaveholders saw this as proof that abolitionists would stop at nothing to further their cause.

Brown was captured in the Armory fire engine house (now called John Brown's Fort) as most of his men lay dead or dying. He was brought to trial at nearby Charles Town and was found guilty of treason, conspiring with slaves to rebel and murder. He was hanged on December 2, 1859. Although John Brown's raid didn't meet his expectations, the trial and execution served to focus the nation's attention on the issue of slavery. It was a major step toward civil war.

Many of the ethereal activities reported in this town can be attributed to this bloody era in our history, as might be expected. The following are some of the infamous hauntings of Harpers Ferry.

The Iron Horse Inn

The Iron Horse Inn is located on Potomac Street in Harpers Ferry. It was built circa 1798 to be the home of the Armory superintendent. During the Civil War, it was occupied, at different periods, by both of the opposing forces in the land. The home was sold after the war to a private individual.

In 1968, Shirley Dougherty opened the building as the Iron Horse Inn. She derived the name from its location near the railroad tracks across the street. Almost immediately, the workers (her son and daughter-in-law) began hearing odd sounds—especially at night. When closing the inn one evening, the young woman was upstairs and heard the doorknob on the door she'd just closed rattling. The door began to shake, as if someone was attempting to force their way through. Fearing a burglar or other intruding miscreant, she froze in place and listened, straining her ears for the tiniest of sounds. Then she heard the unmistakable sound of a large object, or worse—a person—falling down the stairs. *Thump! Thump! Thump!*

She paused but a moment and then raced from the room, convinced that her husband had fallen down the stairs while coming for her. She met her husband as he raced toward her, also assuming the worse—that it was her body he'd heard ricocheting off the steps. The next day, Shirley was told about the experience and was not a believer—until she had the same experience the following night. She was determined no spirit would drive her from the business she'd worked so hard to establish. Nonetheless, her curiosity was piqued about the source of the haunting. Perhaps there was something she could do to help the spirit move on? Eventually, she found a local who was willing to share the town's chatter about her place.

During the Civil War, at a time when the town was occupied by Union troops, a young Confederate spy was sent to infiltrate the area. His mission was to check troop numbers and their movements. It wasn't an uncommon practice to send a young person into the enemy's territory in the belief they'd not be suspected as much as a seasoned veteran might be. As the lad approached the town, he observed guards in the road and lost his nerve. He turned abruptly and hurried back in the direction from which he'd come. The guards yelled at him to stop, but the young boy panicked and fled. He entered a nearby building. He ran up the stairs and attempted to enter a room at the top. He twisted and yanked at the doorknob and then pushed against the door. When the door flew open, he found himself in the very den of his enemies—the room was full of Yankee officers. One officer pulled his revolver and shot the lad in the chest. He fell backward and bounced his way down the stairs, stone dead when he reached the bottom.

The footsteps and stairway sounds are not the only odd occurrences that took place at the Iron Horse. For over two months, on Saturdays at three o'clock in the afternoon, the glass chimney from a kerosene lamp would rise from the lamp and hurl itself across the room. This was witnessed by many observers.

Whatever the ghost's origin might be, it appears it was born under the sign of Aquarius. Several people had water thrown in their face. Five men lunching together said it was as if an entire bucket of water was dumped on them. The building is now an apartment house that is said to be beset by constant turnovers, although one longtime tenant interviewed stated he'd personally observed nothing unexplained in the years he'd lived there.

Shirley Dougherty has passed away, but her interest in local history and ghostly lore gave rise to the local ghost tours that flourish here today.

Hog Alley

The story of Hog Alley is a gruesome one—a tale that highlights man's inhumanity and just how bestial we can be. The alley is a narrow and inconspicuous lane that belies its bloody past. Its name was derived from the fact that the residents once penned up their hogs here. Innocent enough, if you discount having hogs penned up—eating, sleeping and doing all the things that hogs do in the middle of your town. But this was a different time.

View down Hog Alley at Harper's Ferry, West Virginia. *From author's collection.*

Hog Alley sign, Harper's Ferry, West Virginia. *From author's collection.*

During the time of John Brown's raid, Old Tanglefoot Tavern became the assembly area for the town's defenders. Despite the fact that they had access to innumerable weapons, the citizens had little ammunition. They were forced to defend their homes and the arsenal with whatever would fit down the gun barrel. Some local men were leaving the tavern and encountered one of the first attacks. One of the men shot his gun, loaded with iron spikes, and hit Dangerfield Newby in the throat. Dangerfield died instantly. He was the oldest of John Brown's raiders and one of the five Black raiders. He was also the first of Brown's men to die at Harpers Ferry, Virginia. When the fledgling rebellion was defeated, the townsfolk stabbed Dangerfield's body repeatedly. His ears and limbs were severed from his body and then tossed into Hog Alley to be eaten by the hogs.

Many people have since reported seeing the ghost of a tall Black man dressed in period clothing pacing back and forth in the alley. It's said that if you step in front of him, he stops, doffs his hat and disappears. Some say they can see the dripping bloody wound at his throat.

The Civil War Museum

The Civil War Museum and the apartments above it have seen the effects of a grieving mother, even from beyond the grave. A tenant of one of the apartments was said to hear a baby crying on several occasions—usually while the rest of the family slept. One night, with his family away for the evening, the crying baby sounds began in earnest. The man yelled "shut up," and the noise abated. He felt pretty good about this—for about five minutes, but then the crying began anew. "Shut up," he repeated and again the crying stopped. A third time this occurred, followed by the sound of something being thrown out of his bedroom door. Brave or foolhardy, he rushed to investigate. He searched the room and adjacent hallway but saw nothing out of the ordinary. As he turned to leave the room, the crying began again—from behind his bedroom closet. The man was starting to lose his earlier blast of adrenalin and was mentally questioning his decisions to this point. Still, he stepped closer, turned the closet doorknob slowly and, just as slowly, pulled open the door. Nothing was there. He smiled to himself—until the sound of crashing bricks and rocks boomed through the walls. He peered into the darkness but found no damage—nothing to account for the sound of demolition. At this point, he was questioning his own sanity.

After a fitful night sleep, he was leaving the building for work when he met his neighbor.

"What in the world were you doing last night?" the neighbor asked. "It sounded like the walls were caving in."

It's not a matter of record how long the man stayed in the apartment after these events. The source of the sounds and possible haunting remained a mystery for six more years. That's when some reconstruction was done in the nearby Harper House building. A diary was found there that dated to the Civil War times. The diary was written by a young mother. She described in gruesome detail the effects of the war on her town. In her last entry, she tells how the Confederates bombed the town with cannon fire throughout the day. One cannonball struck the wall where her child slept, killing her. Does she still roam those halls in an attempt to comfort her child as the sound of war surrounds them?

SCREAMING JENNY

Screaming Jenny (by the railroad tracks) holds an interesting bit of folklore. The local legend holds that an elderly matron by the name of Jenny resided in a small shack by the railroad tracks. There she'd often be seen scouring the area near the river in search of driftwood to warm her abode. One evening, after retrieving her fuel supply for the night, she stoked the fire. In the process, she ignited the hem of her dress. The flames leapt up her body, and Jenny flew outside alongside the tracks toward the river, screaming for help. So narrow was her focus and so intense her anguish that she didn't see the evening train barreling toward her. Jenny's death was immediate, but it wasn't the end of her tale. Train engineers riding the rails have reported a giant fireball rolling along the tracks, followed by a piercing scream. Are these visions and sounds a reverberation of Jenny's torment?

Saint Peter's Catholic Church

Saint Peter's Catholic Church building was completed in 1833. It is a beacon on a hill, and a more appropriate location for communion with the heavenly hosts can scarcely be imagined. I'm confident that many souls have found salvation within its walls—a citadel to righteousness.

From 1857 to 1867, Saint Peter's found a worthy leader in Father Michael Costello. He was a man of faith and compassion who loved the old church immensely. As fate would dictate, the good father found himself immersed in a battle to save his town and his church when John Brown came to town. St. Peter's was the only church in Harpers Ferry to survive the war. When troops on nearby Maryland Heights would shell the town, Father Costello, being a British subject, would hoist the Union Jack up the steeple. Fearful of an international incident, both sides of the conflict spared the church. Father Michael remained during the raid and throughout the war. The legend is that he so loved his church and his town that he couldn't leave. It's said that his ghost is still seen around the church.

Another apparition has been spied by the front steps of St. Peter's. This ghostly image is dressed as a soldier of the time. During the war, the church was used as a hospital. When this soldier still drew breath, he was brought to the church severely wounded. He waited for attendance by a doctor, but when it seemed he'd bleed to death before that could happen, he was carried inside. As he cleared the threshold of the church, he whispered, "Thank God, I am saved." Many to this day claim to hear those same whispered words as they stand near or enter the church.

Harper House

The site for Harper House was selected by Robert Harper in 1775 for himself and his wife, Rachel. The building was completed in 1782 and is located on a narrow street high atop the hillside in Harpers Ferry. The Harpers ran a ferry service and used the building as a guest house.

One supposed haunting is said to be Rachel Harper. In her old age, she fell to her death from a ladder. Many eyewitnesses report seeing her gazing out of her upstairs bedroom window across the street into the garden below. Legend

Above: Church Ruins, Harper's Ferry, West Virginia. *From author's collection.*

Left: Saint Peter's Church, Harper's Ferry, West Virginia. *From author's collection.*

holds that the elder Mrs. Harper hid money there to avoid paying exorbitant British taxes. If so, she seems to be protecting her hard-earned wealth even in death.

Although the home is inundated with history—both for the famous people who've stayed and lived here and the horrors its walls have witnessed—this last entry's hauntings appear more recent in nature. In modern times, the building served a stint as a residence for state rangers there on training assignments.

One ranger was staying downstairs with his wife at a time when a lady from Washington, D.C., was staying upstairs on a government assignment. The ranger was surprised when the lady asked if she might share their floor and use their spare bedroom as her own. The ranger was perplexed but agreed—the lady was from Washington, D.C., after all. For three weeks, this arrangement worked without incident. At the end of this time, the lady returned to the nation's capital. As she departed, she asked the ranger if he'd ever witnessed anything "strange" in the house. The ranger replied that he had not. Afterward, he thought little more of her question until another ranger asked it again—a year and a half later.

This new ranger reported that he'd seen what he thought was a woman and child dressed in period clothes just outside the entry door. When he opened the door to check on them, they disappeared. He added that he'd seen a man in a top hat and railroad-style pocket watch with a colorful vest wandering the halls who also disappears.

The resident ranger recalled the departing question from the lady in D.C. He decided to risk her ridicule and call to see if she experienced anything that might be described as paranormal. After some difficulty navigating the governmental red tape, he got her on the phone. She described eerily similar visions while staying at the Harper House. The woman and child she also claimed to have seen and watched until they disappeared. But it was the other spirit who haunted her then and still disturbed her dreams. That vision was of a tall man dressed in finery from the late 1800s. He wears a pocket watch and a colorful vest. When she saw him, she didn't know what to make of what was in front of her. Was it a ghost? Could he be a reenactor for some event the Park Service was putting on? She approached him and said hello. The "man" seemed to notice her for the first time and raised his cane over his head as if to strike her. She turned and fled down the hall as he chased her. She could tell from the sound of his footfalls that he was gaining on her. He had almost caught her and then

Harper House is said to be the most haunted building in Harper's Ferry, West Virginia. *From author's collection.*

his steps fell silent. At the safety of her own door, she hazarded a furtive glance down the hall, but no one was there. It was the next morning when she asked the ranger to share his family's quarters.

Harpers Ferry is the headquarters of the resort area that includes the national historic park. The park encompasses approximately three and a half square miles. In 1944, most of the town became part of the National Park Service and is currently maintained as the Harpers Ferry National Historical Park. All areas of the town not within the park are in the federally recognized Harpers Ferry Historic District. The park received national historic park designation in 1963.

The town and the national historical park located here are well worth a visit. The history jumps out at you here, and it's easy to visualize the terror for all involved during John Brown's raid. For a warmer and less bloody historical remembrance, take a short hike to Jefferson's rock and gaze at the view our forefather deemed truly exceptional. The sight is much the same now as it was in Jefferson's time. Hikers will also appreciate the fact that the Appalachian Trail passes through the middle of the town. Harpers

Ferry also has a Wax museum dedicated to Brown's raid. Like many spooky towns it has several ghost tours available to raise your hackles, including the one we attended, Ghost Tours of Harpers Ferry.

8
Brunswick, Maryland

Brunswick is located on the southwest edge of Frederick County, Maryland. It is situated just over forty-five miles upriver from the nation's capital on the Potomac, and six miles east of Harpers Ferry. The population was under six thousand during the last census in 2010.

The area around what we now call Frederick County, Maryland, was once the ancestral home of the Susquehanna Indians. The Susquehannock people lived in longhouses built in walled villages to hamper attack from enemies. In 1728, the first European settlement was built on what would become Brunswick. It was then called Eel Town, because of the Native Americans' fondness for the eels they fished from the Potomac here. A grant to the land was later given to John Hawkins on August 10, 1753. Hawkins sold his rights in 1787 to Leonard Smith, the plat by then called Berlin because of the many Germanic families residing in the area. With an established town on the Eastern Shore by the same name, the postal service changed the name to Barry, Maryland. The last name change occurred in 1890, when the town was incorporated as Brunswick. For lovers of trivia, Patsy Cline (ah, what a voice!) met her husband, Gerald Cline, here while she was singing at the local Moose Lodge.

The Brunswick Heritage Museum was established to preserve the town's history as a hub for the Baltimore and Ohio (B&O) Railroad. It is housed in a building erected circa 1904. The origins of the supposed hauntings here are unknown, neither the cause nor the timeline when they

Frederick County Seal. *Public domain.*

began. It is true that this same building was once the gathering place for the Improved Order of Red Men. (This was a fraternal drinking club born from secret societies from before the American Revolution. Another band of brothers called the Fraternal Order of Eagles also once resided here for the span of several decades.)

Although the basis of the paranormal activity here is purely conjecture, it has been reported at least as long as the museum has been open (1980). Sources in the area claim the "disturbances" reached a fevered pitch during construction of an elevator in 2010. Many have reported strange footsteps, objects being moved around when nobody's in the building and disembodied voices. A woman, described as dressed entirely in white, has been observed walking through the second floor of the building. There were sightings by one individual who once lived in the apartments above the museum. He recalled that as a small child, he'd seen the woman in the white dress and was afraid to sleep alone in the apartment.

It seems odd that a woman is seen here, given the many years the building served as a meetinghouse for two different fraternal organizations. Could she be the wife of one of those men, searching for her husband? Could it be that she is distraught that her husband had not returned home, or is she perturbed thinking her husband overindulged during an evening meeting again? Or perhaps she is the wife of one of the many railroad workers who labored here. As I've found no detailed description of the time period of her clothing, could her haunting be more recent in nature? Is she a relative of one of the crew or passengers killed in the fiery Silver Spring train crash? On February 16, 1996, a MARC commuter train collided with an Amtrak limited passenger train. Eleven people perished in the crash and flames. Their last journey began at the Brunswick station.

Paranormal investigators have captured snippets of spectral conversations here. Their EVPs recorded "have a nice day" and "Smith," perhaps an otherworldly reference to the Dr. Smith who once resided here.

The third floor of the museum was once used as a speakeasy and contained a small stage for entertainment. This has been reported as the focus of some spectral activity as well, although I didn't witness any and could find no one to testify about the paranormal activity on this floor.

Today, Brunswick is an interesting place to visit. Don't miss the chance for a jaunt down the National Park Service C&O Canal or take a MARC train ride. You can book a float downriver with the River and Trail Outfitters and, of course, visit the Brunswick Heritage Museum. There's also the River's Edge Trails, located in the Brunswick Sportsplex. When completed, it will boast a total of five miles open for use.

9
Leesburg, Virginia

Leesburg was built in 1740 and now serves as the county seat of Loudoun County, Virginia. It's located at the base of Catoctin Mountain by the Potomac River. The U.S. census shows this growing community with a population of fifty-two thousand. Its growth can be largely attributed to being only thirty-three miles from the nation's capital, Washington, D.C.

Leesburg also has a very significant history. During the Civil War, Leesburg was the site of the Battle of Ball's Bluff, a significant Confederate victory. The Battle of Mile Hill was fought north of town preceding the occupation by the Army of Northern Virginia prior to the Maryland campaign. Leesburg changed hands several times during the war years.

In the next major U.S. conflict (the War of 1812), Leesburg became the temporary seat of the United States government for a period, as it was forced to flee Washington, D.C., ahead of the British army's advance.

Some of the notable and spookier sites in Leesburg follow.

Ball's Bluff Battlefield Regional Park and National Cemetery

Ball's Bluff Battlefield Regional Park and National Cemetery contains the site of a Civil War battlefield as well as a small U.S. National Cemetery. The park consists of 223 acres. The park offers tours and over seven miles of walking trails.

The 1861 Battle of Ball's Bluff took place here on October 20, 1861. Fifty-four soldiers are buried in the cemetery. Some were killed in the course of the Confederate victory. Many more Union soldiers were drowned during the Union retreat when they were pushed over a bluff into the Potomac. Hundreds surrendered rather than try their luck in the river. Some visitors have claimed that it is haunted by the souls buried there. Wispy apparitions have been observed in visitors' peripheral visions. Others have spotted shadow figures patrolling the scene of their demise or heard ghostly whispers in their ears from unseen entities.

OATLANDS PLANTATION

Oatlands Plantation was once known as a profitable wheat and wool producer. It was a large concern with 3,500 acres in its boundaries. Historical records indicate that as many as seven dozen slaves labored there. The current historic site is reduced to 260 acres.

The manor house was built in 1804 and is currently used as a museum. It is also rumored to be haunted by a few noisy spirits. Doors have been reported as locking on their own. Visitors describe hearing footsteps and disembodied voices when no one is present. Some claim to smell the unexplained scent of roses upstairs. One reported that during a tour of the property, he heard the sound of furniture being rearranged upstairs. After the tour was completed, he inquired about the sounds. The tour guide revealed that nobody was upstairs during the tour—perhaps it was his imagination? The settling of a very old building? Or…?

10
Sterling, Virginia

Sterling is a town located in Loudoun County, Virginia, near the Potomac River and twenty-eight miles from Washington, D.C. It is known for its low crime rate, nice weather, great housing opportunities, good income base and many local amenities.

At the turn of the twentieth century, the Sterling area consisted primarily of large single-family-owned farms that produced cattle for both dairy and meat. The growth of this industry was due to the arrival of the railroad station in 1860. The resultant influx of trade opportunities allowed effective transport of milk, cream and butter to the Washington, D.C. markets. It's estimated that the population at that time (1920–30s) remained at approximately two hundred people.

The town's next major growth spurt occurred with the arrival of the nearby airport. Dulles International Airport (five miles to the south) began initial construction in 1959, and the population soared. The 2010 census reflected a population of nearly twenty-eight thousand people.

During the Civil War, the town felt the effects of the Second Battle of Dranesville (also known as the Ambush at Anker's Shop). This was a small, intense cavalry skirmish that took place between Colonel John Mosby's Confederates and the Captain James Reed's Union troops on February 22, 1864. The battle soon devolved into bloody hand-to-hand combat. Reed was captured, but the Confederate soldier failed to secure the captain's firearm. When the soldier turned away, Captain Reed shot him in the back. Retaliation was swift and deadly. With their commander dead, the Union soldiers retreated. Along with Reed, Mosby's rangers killed twelve others, wounded twenty-five and captured seventy along with one hundred horses. Many others from the Northern army drowned in the Potomac in their haste to escape. Mosby left the field with only five wounded and one killed.

Many of the historic buildings associated with "Old Sterling" are gone now, victims of progressive urban renewal and time. The old grain mill is gone, as is the railway depot. No remnants mark the passage of the blacksmith shop or the many historic barrooms. The "Summer White House" (built in the 1850s) served as a home and hotel for many years. President James Buchanan is said to have brought family members here on weekend escapes from the Washington summers. It was destroyed in a controlled fire in 1989. In 1971, the rundown Sterling Emporium was also burned to the ground by the local fire department. Sterling Hotel shared a similar fate. Perhaps this is why the peculiar experiences some locals and visitors report are not in the form of haunted houses.

One reported an incident that took place on a dirt road outside of Sterling proper. On that warm summer night in a remote area, the local resident observed a young woman who appeared to be dressed as an enslaved person. Having imbibed a few beers, the local was at first unsure of the story that his eyes told. Was some sort of historical reenactment going on and the reenactor lost her way? But again, this was in a very isolated area. It was full dark, and although he felt in no imminent danger, the hairs raised on the back of his neck. He was close enough to observe the woman's worn and dirty clothes. Her hair was disheveled, and shackles adorned her ankles. Did any enactments go so far? The woman took no notice of him as she continued walking down the road. He planted his face in his hands to compose himself and rubbed his eyes. When he looked back to where the woman was last seen, she was gone.

Another nearby resident reported strange happenings in her home: the sounds of footsteps in the dark—in unoccupied rooms, tapping sounds emanating from the unfinished attic, spectral orbs caught during video chats with friends, dark shadows moving through her living room.

There's also a local legend concerning a very young spectral girl. It's said that the girl was mad at her parents and decided to run away from home. When darkness fell, her fears bloomed, and she decided home wasn't so bad after all. As she retraced her steps home, she was struck and killed by a drunk driver. I've found no record of this tragedy, but that doesn't diminish the reports of those who've witnessed the vision of the girl. They feel her sorrow when beholding this forsaken young one walking ahead of them, sobs racking her tiny frame, only to disappear into the night.

Finally, there's the tale of the dark man. It's said that he walks the lonely avenues at night wearing a black overcoat. He continues his walk home every evening, with a cigarette dangling from his lips. He does not react to anyone spotting him, either unaware or feigning ignorance of their presence. He's still intent on finding his way home after the car accident that took his life many years ago.

PART IV

BIG CITY LIGHTS

THIS IS THE SECTION of the river between Maryland and Virginia where the Potomac passes through the most populated section of its length. Great efforts are slowly returning the river to a degree of its historic pristine beauty—far removed from its condition in 1965. That's when President Lyndon B. Johnson called the river here "a national disgrace." Polluted water filled the channel, and bulldozers had filled in and destroyed much of the feeder streams and surrounding wetlands. The river that provides 90 percent of the drinking water to the D.C. metro area was choked with algae and trash. The Clean Water Act of 1972 started the resurgence of the Potomac and other rivers across the country. In 1998, President Bill Clinton designated the Potomac as an American Heritage River. This allowed the river communities to access federal resources to help restore the river for the following five years.

The residents here are a diverse group. The primary employers are the federal government, the military and the host of contractors used by both.

11
Arlington, Virginia

Arlington is an independent city in Arlington County, Virginia. As of the 2010 census, the population was nearly 140,000. It is located along the western bank of the Potomac River and is approximately seven miles south of downtown Washington, D.C. It is the second-largest principal city of the Washington metropolitan area.

The entire Arlington County area was once a part of the nation's capital. The county was originally part of the ten-mile square surveyed in 1791 for the nation's capital. From 1801 to 1847, what are now Arlington and a portion of the city of Alexandria were known as Alexandria County, District of Columbia. In 1847, at the request of the local residents, Congress gave Alexandria County back to the Commonwealth of Virginia. The driving forces behind the request was the divisions over slavery and the lack of voting rights for the residents of the District.

One of the first battles of the Civil War occurred at Arlington Mill, Virginia, on June 1, 1861. In the dark of that fateful night, a small squad consisting of nine Virginia soldiers fired on the First Michigan Volunteer Infantry. The U.S. troops were on picket duty. The battle was a brief affair resulting in the death of one Northern soldier and the wounding of another. The Virginians suffered one wounded. Although the battle seems insignificant—especially for those times, it made the North aware of how vulnerable it was, even in its own "backyard." Regrettably, the historic Arlington Mill was destroyed by fire in 1920. A new community center opened on the same site in September 2013.

Arlington is home to the well-known Tomb of the Unknown Soldier. It also houses the lesser-known Tomb of the Civil War Unknowns. The bloody slaughter brought about by the Civil War soon used up all available space in the area's existing cemeteries. Many of the war's early battles were fought here. U.S. Army quartermaster general Montgomery Meigs proposed that the Arlington House property, occupied since the spring of 1861, should be used as a burial ground. This home belonged to Confederate general Robert E. Lee and was selected in part for its political expediency to ensure that Lee would never again return to his home. (The Supreme Court found that the estate was "illegally confiscated" in 1864 and ordered it returned to the Lee family. They sold it back to the government.) Arlington House overlooks the Potomac River and the National Mall in Washington, D.C.

The Civil War Unknowns Monument is a burial vault and memorial that was dedicated in 1866. It rests on top of a vault beneath which lie the remains of 2,111 soldiers. Their mortal remains were gathered from the fields of Bull Run in Virginia and along the route to the Rappahannock River. Of the dead, 1,800 were retrieved from the carnage at Bull Run alone. The 400 others were found scattered across battlefields and trenches within an approximate twenty-five-mile radius of Washington, D.C. This was the first memorial at Arlington to be dedicated to soldiers killed in battle and whose remains were unidentified. As such, both the identity and, in many cases, the side for which they fought are unknown.

With some of the above background in mind, let's take our own haunted tour.

The Febrey-Kincheloe House

The Febrey-Kincheloe House was built as a country home and stood for more than a century. Ernest Febrey constructed the grand home in the 1890s. Some years later (after daughter Margaret Febrey passed away), the Kincheloe family bought the house. In 1947, when Mr. Kincheloe died, his wife transitioned the home for use as a rest home for Washington dignitaries called the Crestwood Sanitarium. Its final transition was when the property was acquired by the Overlee Community Association in 1967 and a pool was built on the premises. In 2012, the association made the decision to demolish the historic home. This is when the reports of hauntings began.

Clubhouse caretakers and staff reported hearing music and laughing late into the night. Upon investigation, the sounds would immediately stop.

Some of the caretakers attributed the unseen source of the noises to the old building's bones settling. Some others, with a different view of the afterlife, attributed it to the home's time as a sanitarium and the horrors of a broken mind that might survive even death.

Before the Febrey-Kincheloe House was sold, contractors and realtors spoke of seeing a strangely dressed girl standing by the basement stairs. In 2012 (when the old building was demolished), construction workers at the Overlee Community Center reported that they were not alone—they would often see a young girl dressed in Victorian-era clothing climbing through the construction/demolition rubble. She'd walk through with a familiarity that suggested she knew the site well and knew exactly where she was going—even though she seemed in no hurry to get there.

Who was this wandering spectral child? Local tradition holds that she is none other than young Margaret Febrey. Margaret died in January 1913 of a spinal infection called Pott's disease. While the noisy and playful spirits that inhabit the clubhouse are secretive things, never seen and silent when approached, this is not so for our Miss Margaret. Perhaps due to her youth when passing, Margaret is not at all wary of the living. She's been seen around the property on many occasions. Visitors have even reported having conversations with her. She's been seen poolside, and swimmers have reported speaking to a girl in a gray Victorian dress. She is said to be especially friendly to young children.

ARLINGTON HALL

Arlington Hall is located close to the intersection of Arlington Boulevard and South George Mason Drive. It was originally founded as a private post-secondary educational institution for women by Dr. William Martin in 1927.

By the mid-1930s, the school fell on hard times financially, and in 1940, it was converted into a nonprofit. A few years later, the U.S. Army usurped possession of the facility under the War Powers Act. During World War II, Arlington Hall was used by the U.S. Intelligence Service as one of two primary cryptography operations in Washington. The concentration was on Japanese code systems.

Arlington Hall might no longer be a home to the top-secret codebreakers, but it still retains its shadowy nature, with those who've left this life behind.

Odd enough was the Civil War period shell that was found under a hallway during a refurbishment in 2008, but the unexplained here isn't only that of the natural world. Unexplained noises in the night—more robust than just the settling of old timbers, are often heard by occupants in the peaceful hours of night. Footsteps are heard echoing on the hard floors above and then transitioning to more muffled steps as the carpeted area is reached. Brave and inquisitive souls who've allowed their curiosity to overcome their caution say they've come upon a young woman in a flowery print dress, attired as if attending a social occasion, stepping into the ladies' room. She double-checks her look in the mirror, turns and, without a word, disappears.

It's unknown who this wandering soul might be or why she clings to her former life. Is she one of the many young women who attended the balls held at Arlington Hall Junior College for Women? Was she perhaps jilted by one of the men who labored away at breaking the Japanese codes during World War II?

12

WASHINGTON, DISTRICT OF COLUMBIA

Washington, D.C., is the capital of the United States of America. It was founded in 1790 as the seat of government for our new and independent country. It was named after our first president and founding father, George Washington. Washington is located on the Potomac River, where it borders Maryland and Virginia.

The city's storied history stretches back in time before its renaming in 1791. Many small tribes of the Piscataway people (also known as the Conoy) called these lands along around the Potomac River home, before the first Europeans stepped foot here in the seventeenth century. Conflicts soon erupted between the two disparate peoples, though, and the Conoy sought a more peaceful environment. In 1699, most of the Natives deserted the area and settled the land around present-day Point of Rocks, Maryland.

The U.S. Constitution required a federal district under the exclusive jurisdiction of Congress, and as a result, the district is not a part of any U.S. state. It was originally created from lands donated by the states of Maryland and Virginia. (In 1846, Congress returned the land originally ceded by Virginia back to the state at its request).

During the War of 1812, British forces attacked the city. The attack continued for two days, from August 24 to 25, 1814. The Capitol (it was under construction at that time), the Treasury and the White House were burned to the ground after the contents of each was looted.

Washington, D.C., is one of the most visited cities in the United States. It is estimated that more than twenty million people visit annually and with

District of Columbia pre–Civil War. *From the Ghosts of D.C. collections.*

little wonder. Its attractions include far more than the trappings of the federal government. The National Mall is located here. It's an open-air park in downtown and the home of the United States Capitol. It's known for being the location of political protests, concerts, festivals and presidential inaugurations. The Washington Monument and the Jefferson Pier are near the center of the mall. Also here are the Vietnam Veterans Memorial, the National World War II Memorial, the Lincoln Memorial Reflecting Pool and the Korean War Veterans' Memorial.

World-class museums are also located here. The Smithsonian Institution is the largest research and museum compound in the world. Its collections are open to the public free of charge. The most popular of the scattered Smithsonian satellite museums is the National Museum of Natural History, but many other Smithsonian museums and galleries are found along the mall.

South of the mall is the Tidal Basin. This is where the beautiful rows of Japanese cherry trees are seen. These three thousand trees were gifted to the city in 1912 by the government of Japan. The trees spurred the annual Cherry Blossom Festival from late March to early April. Several other memorials are also located here, including the Franklin Delano Roosevelt Memorial, the Jefferson Memorial, the Martin Luther King Jr. Memorial and the District of Columbia War Memorial.

Left: Washington monument under construction in 1883. *From the Smithsonian Archives.*

Below: Aerial View of National Mall under construction (circa 1930). *By permission of Cornell University Library.*

In a city with so much history—much of it violent in nature—it's a given that Washington would nurture paranormal activity. No matter what your opinion is of the politicians or the extensive bureaucracy associated with our nation's capital, one thing is for sure, at least the hauntings here will not disappoint.

FORT LESLEY J. MCNAIR ARMY BASE

Fort Lesley J. McNair Army Base in Washington, D.C., is an army facility on a peninsula at the confluence of the Anacostia and Potomac Rivers. It has a history that spans two hundred years. On July 7, 1865, Mary Elizabeth Jenkins Surrat was executed here. She was the first woman executed by the United States government, after she was convicted of conspiracy in Abraham Lincoln's assassination.

Some years earlier, after her husband's death in 1862, Surratt had to manage his estate. Unable to do so without help, she moved to her townhouse in Washington, D.C., which she ran as a boardinghouse. The home was located a few blocks from Ford's Theatre, where the assassination of President Lincoln occurred. The house was reputed to be a meeting place for Southern sympathizers. It is here that John Wilkes Booth first laid the groundwork for the assassination of the president. More than any other hard evidence against her, it was Surratt's association with Booth that sealed her fate.

Early in the day when Lincoln was shot, Booth passed a package to Mary Surratt with directions for its delivery to her tenant John Lloyd, who leased her tavern in Surrattsville, Maryland. It is said that this was not an unusual request and that Surratt already had intentions of heading there to collect her rents. After the assassination, confusion ensued over the package's contents. Both binoculars for Lloyd and weapons for the two killers have been suggested. When the police later questioned Lloyd about their encounter, he failed to mention anything of significance. He further denied that Booth and David Herold had ever visited the tavern. When questioned later in the proceedings, he claimed that Surratt told him to have whiskey and the "shooting irons" (hidden in the tavern loft) ready for Booth and Herold that fateful evening.

Louis Weichmann was initially arrested as one of the conspirators. He'd accompanied Surratt to the tavern but was released after he testified against

Print of Pennsylvania Avenue toward the Capitol published between 1811 and 1814 (before the British burned). *Unknown artist. From the Library of Congress. Contributor Benjamin Henry Latrobe.*

her. He later claimed that the government coerced him into testifying. For the remainder of his life, he claimed his dishonesty at the trial ate at his conscience.

Lewis Powell, a conspirator who was hanged with Surratt, proclaimed her innocence to his executioner until the moment of his death, as did Mary herself.

The U.S. government had never executed a woman, and many anticipated a reprieve from President Andrew Johnson. As a result, the execution was delayed until the afternoon. Soldiers were stationed along the entire thoroughfare from the White House to the fort in anticipation of the forthcoming pardon, but none came. The debate continues to this day about how involved Mary actually was and if the punishment fit the crime—especially given the contradictory nature of the accounts and charges against her. Mary is buried at Mount Olivet Cemetery.

Since her death, there have been many sightings of what's thought to be Mary Surratt's ghost. Most notable is a hooded figure dressed entirely in black and bound hand and foot—just as Surratt had been at the time of her execution. This figure often appears more "solid" than at other times—especially around the anniversary of her death, July 7, 1865. Some of the children of the soldiers stationed there have informed their parents that a "lady in black" often plays with them, only to vanish as quickly as she appears. Perhaps Mary seeks a final justice in death that was unknown to her in life?

The White House

The White House was first occupied by President John Adams and his wife, Abigail, in 1800. Despite having no running water at the time, apparently Abigail loved her new digs. Her ghost has been seen since shortly after her death in 1818. The apparition had her arms extended as she did in life while carrying laundry into the drafty East Room to dry. These sightings are often followed by the smell of soap and damp clothing. (*Clairscent* is when someone experiences an aroma that's not from the person's physical world. It is one of the rarer forms of a "haunting.") During William Taft's administration, his household staff claimed to often spot Mary as she walked through the walls.

It's well known that the ghost most encountered at the White House is Abraham Lincoln. Too many notable and credible personages have reported such an experience, that it would be impossible to dismiss out of hand. The very first person to report seeing Lincoln's ghost was First Lady Grace Coolidge. She observed Lincoln standing in the Yellow Oval Room gazing out the window across the grounds toward the Potomac.

Eleanor Roosevelt said she felt Lincoln's presence on many occasions throughout the White House. Their family dog, Fala, would bark for no reason at what she was convinced was Lincoln's ghost. (Animals and children are said to have a clearer connection to the spirit world.)

Many notable guests have reported hearing Lincoln's footsteps in the hall outside the Lincoln bedroom. Lillian Rogers Parks stated in her autobiography, *My Thirty Years Backstairs at the White House*, that she had heard them. Margaret Truman, daughter of President Harry S. Truman, said she heard a specter rapping at the door of the Lincoln Bedroom when she stayed there, and she felt confident the ghostly treads belonged to none other than Honest Abe.

A knocking at bedroom doors at odd hours of the night have been referenced repeatedly over the years. President Truman stated that he was once awakened by taps at his door when sleeping in the Lincoln Bedroom. The list of political celebrities who stated emphatically that they'd personally witnessed an apparition of the former president include Winston Churchill and President Theodore Roosevelt. It seems Lincoln's specter was particularly active during the Franklin D. Roosevelt administration. Several claimed to have seen Lincoln's spirit during that period. It's said that FDR's personal valet ran screaming from the White House after seeing Lincoln's ghost.

Most famous of the Lincoln appearances (and a personal favorite) was in 1942. That's when Queen Wilhelmina of the Netherlands visited. Late at night, she stood to investigate footsteps outside of her assigned White House quarters. At a knock on the door (not sure why the queen was without her valet), she pulled open the door, and there stood Abe Lincoln. He was dressed in his renowned top hat with a long frock coat over his shoulders. Without further ado, and with total disregard to political decorum, the queen fainted.

In the early 1980s, Tony Savoy, the White House operations foreman, reported spotting Lincoln sitting in a chair at the top of the stairs. Sources indicate that this was the last reported sighting of our sixteenth president—or at least the last one reported to the public.

THE UNITED STATES CAPITOL

The United States Capitol is considered by many to be one of the most haunted buildings in Washington (and that's quite an accomplishment). In fact, the first sighting of a "spirit" reported here was before the Capitol was even completed in 1860. But there are several ghosts that are said to date to this period, as there were many tragedies associated with the building's construction. It seems that one spirit feels his work is still not completed. His otherworldly tale began after a fatal fall during the building of the rotunda. His ghostly image has been seen floating beneath the dome to this day—with a tray of woodworking tools clutched in his arms. Yet another is the resident (and dead) stonemason. The details of his demise are uncertain. It's said by some that he was murdered by a coworker, while others support the more mundane cause of death—a collapsing masonry wall. He's often seen flitting about in the Old Senate chambers or passing through a basement wall beneath it.

Former president John Quincy Adams (and later Representative Adams, as he was at the time of this story) suffered a stroke in the House chamber on February 21, 1848, and was moved to the speaker's office. Adams's doctor advised that his condition was too critical to allow him to be moved. Two days later, on February 23, he died there. Many people claim to have heard Adams's ghost denouncing slavery late at night in National Statuary Hall. One staff member claimed that while standing at the former location of Adams's desk, he'd heard Adams's disembodied whisper.

Another memorable event that echoes with the paranormal involves Representative William P. Taulbee (a congressman from Kentucky) and Charles E. Kincaid (a *Louisville Times* reporter). Kincaid accused Taulbee of adultery and involvement in a Patent Office scandal. Whether unfounded or not, the accusations put an end to Taulbee's political career. On February 28, 1890, the two men met again at the Capitol. Taulbee assaulted the much smaller man by tweaking his nose in an aggressive (and very demeaning) fashion. Kincaid rushed home for his pistol. He found Taulbee on a marble staircase that led from the House chamber to the dining room. He shot Taulbee just below the left eye, and Taulbee died two weeks later. Kincaid claimed self-defense and was acquitted of all charges. Some journalists, perhaps more superstitious than others, claim that when they slipped on these steps, Taulbee's ghost briefly appeared.

Then there's the story of the Demon Cat. This brought back memories of the "mascat" of the Shepherdstown's Mystery Walk. Unlike that friendly feline, however, this supernatural kitty only seems to associate with humans when it prophesizes a disaster. It's said to creep through halls of Congress before a national tragedy or to mark a change in the occupant of the White House. It was first reported in the early years of the nineteenth century. In 1862, a nightwatchman took at potshot at it. Other watchmen over the years have reported the shadowy prowling cat, as have the Capitol Police. It made its appearance just before the Lincoln assassination, again just before the October 1929 stock market crash and yet again before the assassination of President John F. Kennedy. The cat also makes an occasional guest appearance at Washington's Tomb.

Many more federal buildings and personal homes are said to be haunted in our nation's capital. The list is so extensive that it is beyond the scope of this book. I'd be remiss not to list some of the more notable ones. Ghost hunters and lovers of the macabre would do well to check out some of the following.

Lafayette Square

Lafayette Square is said to be haunted by Philip Barton Key II. He was the son of Francis Scott Key. In 1858, Key began a torrid affair with Teresa Sickles, the wife of his friend Daniel Sickles. Sickles learned of the affair and spotted Key in Lafayette Square with his wife. Sickles rushed Key, drawing his pistol as he ran, and shot the unarmed man three times—even while Key pleaded for his life. Eyewitnesses claim that Key haunts Lafayette Square and can be seen on dark nights near where he was shot.

Independence Avenue Southwest

The spirits of slaves are also said to haunt a portion of Independence Avenue Southwest. Two of the city's largest slave markets were located here. Here a modest, two-story yellow house concealed a very large basement. In that basement, horrors awaited those misfortunates who found themselves held captive. The enslaved people were chained to walls in windowless rooms. A small yard was surrounded by a high brick wall. This provided space for the training and selling of slaves. This was the infamous Williams Slave Pen. Nearby was the other large slave market, known as the Robey Slave Pen. On windless nights, witnesses have reported hearing the clinking of chains and screams all along this section of Independence Avenue where the slave pens operated.

Cassandra Chew

Cassandra Chew bought the Old Stone House home in 1767. She was a wealthy widow who soon set about enlarging the house. A kitchen was constructed in 1767, and the addition of a second floor began the same year. The third floor was added in 1790. In 1953, the building was purchased by the federal government.

A large number of spirits are claimed to inhabit the small house, verified by visitors and residents alike. Although many spirits have been reported here over the years, the source of the haunting or the tragedy that led to their continued presence here remains unknown. What horrors might have occurred over the home's two-hundred-year history?

There are stories of a woman who stands by the burning fireplace and an obese lady who loiters on the staircase. Some others insist on visitations by a man with long blond hair and wearing a blue jacket, as well as a man wearing short pants and long stockings. There's a man wearing colonial-era clothing who stands motionless in the master bedroom and also appears on the second floor. The laughter of young children has been heard when no children are in attendance. But one spirit remnant is not so aloof or peaceful. Visitors have said they felt his strong hands around their necks choking them, and he's known to shove others. He's been nicknamed "George," and his presence is often made known by cold spots in the room. Folks who've reported encounters with this spirit say he leaves them with feelings of dread. These are but a sample of the spirits residing at the Old Stone House. They were made well-known after their mention in Sandi Wilson's short crime story, "The Blonde in Black."

13
Alexandria, Virginia

Alexandria is a heavily developed independent city in the Commonwealth of Virginia. According to the 2010 census, the population was nearly 140,000. It is located along the west bank of the Potomac River and lies approximately seven miles south of downtown Washington, D.C.

Archaeologists conclude that there was a succession of indigenous peoples once living here and estimate that they first populated the Chesapeake tidewater region between three thousand and ten thousand years ago. As early as the fourteenth century, Algonquian-speaking peoples established small towns throughout the Potomac's drainage.

John Smith encountered many of them during his historic explorations beginning in 1608. Members of the Powhatan confederacy, as well as the Piscataway (also known as the Conoy), were known to Smith on this visit. He also noted the existence of a Native settlement named Assaomeck. It was mapped out as being near the south bank of what is now Hunting Creek in present-day Alexandria.

Alexandria is known for its Old Town. Well-maintained brick sidewalks frame the eighteenth- and nineteenth-century buildings here, along with the many boutiques and specialty shops.

Some of the first fatalities of the Civil War occurred in Alexandria. After the Battle of Fort Sumter, Union troops occupied the city on May 24, 1861. The troops landed at King Street on the Potomac. A short distance away, a detachment of the New York Fire Zouaves removed a large Confederate flag

Alexandria waterfront taking on slaves. *From broadside published by the American Anti-Slavery Society.*

displayed on the roof of the Marshall House Inn, which was visible from the White House. While descending from the roof, a Colonel Ellsworth was shot dead by the proprietor, James W. Jackson. In retribution, one of the soldiers immediately shot and killed Jackson. This fomented strong passions on both sides of the Mason-Dixon line. Ellsworth was honored as a martyr to the Union cause to much fanfare in the North. The South was equally incensed. They saw it as Jackson being murdered for defending his own property. Alexandria remained under military occupation for the duration of the war.

THE WAR OF 1812

The Civil War isn't the only wartime period that left its forbidding brand on this area of Virginia and contributed to the collection of supernatural stories. During the War of 1812, for example, Alexandria was ransacked by British troops. On August 29, 1814, Alexandrians wiped the sleep from their eyes and stared out their windows at 138 guns of the British squadron "but a few hundred yards from the wharves, and the houses so situated as they might have been laid in ashes in a few minutes." The city surrendered without a fight. In accordance with the terms of surrender, the Brits looted stores and warehouses of all naval stores, along with flour, tobacco, sugar and wine. Like other towns in the path of the British, everything of value (that could be carried off) was taken. Unlike some others, the terms were honored, and Alexandria was spared the torch that ravished many towns during that war. Without this compromise, there would be no Old Town to visit today.

In the course of the town's panic when the ships approached, two British spies were captured and hanged. Public executions were normally held on Market Square, but in a fury at the state of their town and the invading troops, a house on Prince Street served to do the deed. When the British aggressors entered the house, they found the bodies hanging from the rafters. Many people, including some past occupants of the home, say they are still there.

Gadsby's Tavern

Gadsby's Tavern is a well-known complex of historic buildings at the corner of North Royal and Cameron Streets in Old Town Alexandria, Virginia. Founding fathers were known to dine at Gadsby's. The original tavern building (circa 1785) now also houses the 1792 City Tavern and Hotel and the "new" hotel section, which was added in 1878.

For many of the founding fathers of our country, the tavern was a favored meeting place. Some of the more notable regulars there include George Washington, John Adams, Thomas Jefferson, James Madison, James Monroe and the Marquis de Lafayette. George Washington celebrated a few of his birthday bashes here and continued visiting the tavern after his retirement from political life. Not many years after, the first reports of hauntings began.

Sometime in 1816, a young woman arrived in town and was soon thereafter afflicted with cholera. Although only about ten cases of cholera are reported in the United States a year these days (and half of those are contracted overseas), it was a very serious condition in the 1800s. The young woman doubtless obeyed her doctor's instructions for a cure. Those would have included avoiding drafts and dressing in warm, dry clothes; keeping the fires

Gadsby's Tavern at left. Spire of city hall, circa 1940. *From the Charles W. Cushman collection.*

high and the room dry; avoiding cold beverages; and not getting wet. This might have led to some cures or perhaps the patient's own immune system proved up to the task—but not for the young lady in question. Severe watery diarrhea, accompanied by vomiting, quickly led to dehydration, and in short order, the concerned husband became a grieving widower.

For some odd reason (that wasn't disclosed), the couple never revealed the family's surname. It's been speculated that the family was wanted in another jurisdiction for some nefarious deed or that the young couple had fled from the disapproval of their families back home. Whatever the reason for their reticence, the young wife's tombstone stands in the Wilkes Street Cemetery Complex engraved with the words: "To the memory of a female stranger."

The story goes that the husband did not wait to see his wife laid to rest but left after leaving a bank note to cover the cost of the interment. The local citizens who erected this monument to the unknown were surprised when the bank note used to pay for her memorial was found to be a forgery—the signatory did not exist. Many are even more surprised when visiting the site. Some claim the unknown lady haunts it to this day. Many have reported seeing shadows pass suddenly over her grave as a chill runs down their spine.

Some of the staff at Gadsby's Tavern, however, feel the unknown victim remains where she died—in the upstairs room that she and her husband rented. They've reported a mysterious candle that sometimes appears from nowhere—in the very room where she died. There are others who report apparitions and phantom footsteps on the stairs. On occasion, the poor soul is heard crying—longing for her husband's return or in mourning for the life she'd barely begun?

Fairfax Street Ice Cream Shop

Fairfax Street Ice Cream Shop is the site of another series of unexplained sightings in this historic town. In the mid-1800s, the shop was used as a home and was owned by the Schafer family.

The Schafer family's twenty-six-year-old daughter, Laura, was engaged to marry a soldier. It was scheduled for a beautiful early summer day in June 1868. The night before this blessed event, the Schafers planned an early bedtime in anticipation of the full day ahead of them but persuaded Laura to model her wedding dress before retiring for the evening.

After the family's requisite "ohs and ahs" of admiration, Laura helped her grandmother to bed. One can assume the older lady favored her granddaughter with some sage marital advice, and soon thereafter, Laura crossed the hallway to her own room.

As she closed the door to her room, I wonder if the pre-marital jitters overcame her? Or was it some warning her grandmother passed along to her? It's said that the high humidity swelled the door jambs in the house, so it may have happened as she attempted to force the door closed. It could be as simple as a moment of clumsiness, but the kerosene lantern she carried fell to the floor. Kerosene splashed across the floor and up the floor-length dress. A fiery inferno followed the fuel up her dress and swallowed Laura in flame.

No doubt, she panicked, and the sounds of her screams were heard throughout the house. She pulled at the bedroom door, but it would not open. Finally, in anguish, she snatched at the door with all of her might, and it flew open. The rush of air increased the intensity of the flames just as her brother arrived to extinguish them. Despite his efforts, Laura later died from her burns on what was to be her wedding day. Her funeral was held days after at 11:00 a.m. in the family's parlor.

Much of this story can be verified in the archives of the now-defunct *Alexandria Gazette*, but that's not the end of Laura Schafer's tale. Many visitors to this site claim that she still haunts the building. There are reports of a woman weeping when the clock strikes eleven. Other people have testified to objects moving in unoccupied rooms or relocated from where they were known to have been left.

An interactive personality spirit is a deceased person, usually a family member, but often a historical figure associated with a building. They have many ways to make the living aware of their presence. They are the spirits we often see in our peripheral vision or even fully visible to the naked eye.

They can touch things (even you) or give off odors like roses or tobacco smoke. Experts say that this type of ghost retains its former personality from its time as a corporal being.

It was amazing to hear of the quantity of reported hauntings from the research and interviews for this "Big City Lights" section. The surface has only been scratched here, but unlike the spirits who remain after their time among the living ends, it's time now to move on.

PART V

THE COASTAL PLAIN

GEOGRAPHICALLY, THE COASTAL PLAIN is a region of low relief along the East Coast of the United States. The province is bordered on the west by the Atlantic Seaboard Fall Line and the piedmont plateau and to the east by the Atlantic Ocean.

The province's average elevation is less than nine hundred meters above sea level and extends some fifty to one hundred kilometers inland from the ocean. The coastal plain is normally wet with its many rivers, marshes and swamplands. There are no hills or mountains in this region of the Potomac Valley. It is composed primarily of sedimentary rock and sediments and is chiefly used for agriculture.

14
Mount Vernon, Virginia

Mount Vernon is an American landmark and renowned as the former plantation of our nation's first president, George Washington, and his wife, Martha. The estate is located on the banks of the Potomac River in Fairfax County, Virginia. Prince George's County, Maryland, is located directly across the river. The Washington family first purchased land in the area around 1674. Around 1734, the family embarked on an expansion of the estate, which George continued. In 1761, he became the sole master of the manor.

The mansion was constructed of wood by George Washington's father, Augustine, around 1734. George expanded the house twice, in the late 1750s and again in the 1770s. It remained his home for the rest of his life. After his death in 1799, the home place progressively declined from insufficient funds and inattention. In 1858, the Mount Vernon Ladies' Association saved the historic home from ruin, acquiring it along with part of the surrounding property and restoring it to its original glory.

Mount Vernon was designated a National Historic Landmark in 1960 and is listed in the National Register of Historic Places. Still owned and maintained by the Mount Vernon Ladies' Association, it is open every day of the year.

The historic significance of the property lends credence to what some proclaim is one of the most haunted locations in Virginia. It certainly has to be near the top of the list, given the number of spooky tales and sightings associated with the site.

The following account was reported in the *New York World* newspaper in 1890:

> *Of course, the most interesting of all the bedrooms is the one belonging to the immortal George and in which he died. In it is the original four-poster bed whereon Washington passed his last moments.*
>
> *This historic chamber is haunted; of that there would seem to be little doubt. Many people within recent years have slept in it, and they declare that they were awed by the viewless presence of the nation's first President. They deny earnestly that the notion is based on imagination. Few of these temporary occupants have been able to get any sleep. Obviously, it is one thing to see a ghost, and quite another thing to feel one—to be aware of the nearness of a strange and brooding specter. They all agree that Washington visits his chamber in the still watches of the night.*
>
> *Mrs. William Beale and a friend of hers spent a night at Mount Vernon. At their own request, they were permitted to occupy Washington's bedroom. In the middle of the night, they were awakened by the sputtering of their candle. They had had lighted one surreptitiously and were burning it in the middle of a basin of water.*
>
> *Fancied they saw a spook. It went out with a noise, and they began to feel alarmed. Mrs. Beale said to her friend: "You are on the side of the bed where Washington died!" The other replied: "No, I'm not; he died on your side!" Finally, they decided that the question was doubtful, and there was no more sleep for them that night. They got up dressed themselves, and sat around until morning, scared by every squeak of the windows and at one moment were sure they heard Washington's sward clank distinctly in a corner.*

Another often-reported sighting involves the "woman on the stairs." This apparition was first reported around 1980 by a historical character interpreter. While at her station in the Central Passage, something caught her eye. In her report, she stated she'd witnessed the figure of an unidentified woman dressed in eighteenth-century clothing on the stairs. The figure was carrying a large punch bowl filled with a flower arrangement. The figure disappeared upon reaching the bottom of the staircase.

On another occasion, a worker at the mansion observed another supernatural occurrence. It was a particularly active, crowded day at the site, and the area in question wasn't part of the public tour. She was a bit surprised then when she heard someone in the room behind her. Thinking a visitor had snuck into the area by going under the rope barricades, she entered the Little Parlor to ask them to leave. Much to her surprise, she found an old gentleman sitting there. He sported a large mustache and was dressed in early-twentieth-century clothing. His sleeves were rolled up and fastened with period garter bands.

The man shouted, "What the hell is going on here?" He nodded in the direction of the noise generated by a school group passing nearby.

"I'll try to quiet them down," the shocked worker said. With that assurance, the apparition disappeared. She later identified the gentleman from an antique portrait. She claimed it was Colonel Harrison Howell Dodge, Mount Vernon's director for about fifty years until his death in the late 1930s.

Yet another character interpreter described one of her experiences in 2017:

> *I've worked at Mount Vernon on and off since 2004. I most recently returned in January 2017. The estate was abuzz with the latest spooky story. On December 15, 2016, some strange sounds were heard coming from the third floor, and there had been reports of the temperature dropping by twenty degrees. When the tale was shared with me, I was determined to see if it would happen again.*
>
> *On December 14, the anniversary of the general's death, I was on the third floor waiting for some haunting, but nothing happened. However, when I returned the next night, the vibe in the area had changed. Upon looking into the southwest bedchamber, I noticed an electric candle was on. "That's strange," I thought, "it was dark last night." Had Collections come and turned it on? Not likely; the third floor isn't open to the public. Then it hit me. George Washington died on December 14, 1799, and the next day, Martha Washington shut up the bedroom they shared. And moved to the southwest bedchamber. Apparently, she's still marking that sad day.*

Haunted tales of ghostly encounters have occurred throughout the mansion's history (certainly since George's death) and continue to the present day. In the late nineteenth century, spiritualism gained favor, and the result was volumes of ghost stories involving George Washington.

One story made popular in the press at the time was written by a Boston politician, Josiah Quincy Jr. The book was based on Quincy's collection of journals and letters. *Figures of the Past from the Leaves of Old Journals* was published posthumously in 1883. Included in the work were Quincy's remembrances of his father. One story detailed the experiences his father encountered during a visit to Mount Vernon.

Quincy's father, Josiah Quincy III, was also a prominent Massachusetts politician. He served in the U.S. House of Representative from 1805 to 1813, and while serving in Congress, he visited Mount Vernon to meet with Bushrod Washington, George Washington's nephew. Bushrod was the inheritor of Mount Vernon and a Supreme Court justice. Josiah Jr.'s story detailed a distinctly spooky social call.

In the spring of 1806, Quincy arrived at Mount Vernon, intending on spending the night as a guest. In the *Figures of the Past* narrative, Quincy Jr. admitted that he was in Washington, D.C., at the time and was too young to recall the actual event. While the accuracy of much of Quincy Jr.'s book might be best described as historical fiction, this particular story was one that he claimed was "constantly referred to in the family circle." And that this particular tale was "my father's only ghost story."

When Quincy the elder arrived at Mount Vernon, Washington's nephew allocated him his uncle's "bedchamber" for the night—the very room in which George Washington had died. With a dramatic literary flourish, Quincy Jr. explained that "Judge Washington" gave mention to the fact that in that room, "an interview with Washington had been granted to some of its former occupants." The author wrote that his father "pondered upon the possibility that he might be found worthy to behold the glorified spirit of him who was so revered by his countrymen." It is very interesting to note and is a testament to President Washington that nearly a century after his death, even his specter was held in such high regard.

It would seem that his father did prove "worthy," as some time during the night, the apparition of George Washington was seen. Quincy Jr. gives few further details of this visitation, whether to preclude the mocking of his contemporaries or because, in his words, if he gave more details, he would have to consult an "expert in cerebral illusions." He did stipulate that his father's recall of the visitation was perfect and that his father "believed that brain action…was at times set up in us by friends no longer in the flesh, and that his own life had been guided by these mysterious influences."

15

Occoquan, Virginia

Occoquan is a town in Prince William County, Virginia. The population was 934 during the 2010 census. The town is a suburb of Washington, D.C., and is adjacent to Woodbridge. The name *Occoquan* is derived from an Algonquian word, meaning "at the end of the water." The indigenous people inhabited the area and relied on the river for their staples and transportation and as a trade route.

Early in the 1600s, Captain John Smith explored the Occoquan River. In 1608, when the first Europeans reached Northern Virginia, the Tauxenent tribe (also known by the English as the "Dogues") had its main village at the mouth of the Occoquan River. The tribe was closely allied with its neighbors the Piscataway (located across the Potomac River in what is now Maryland). The local chief was called a Tayac and was subservient to the "emperor" located in Prince Georges County, Maryland.

By 1765, Anglo-American colonists established an industrial settlement at Occoquan with gristmills and tobacco warehouses. During the Civil War, the post office passed letters and packages between North and South. Settlements and clearing of the land created river silting that reduced shipping traffic and ended its days as a port, as did the swing from river transportation to the new railroads.

The town today is renowned as a restored artists' community. There's a variety of shops, outdoor dining, a town boat dock and more (including ghost walks). A number of structures in town are part of the Occoquan Historic District listed in the National Register of Historic Places. Some are rumored to be haunted.

Occoquan Inn

Occoquan Inn was built in 1810. It now serves the Occoquan community as D'Rocco's, a restaurant renowned for its fine Italian cuisine, but that's not all it's known for. The apparition of a Native American man has been reported here. Local legend has it that the man was enamored of the original inn owner's wife, and he was shot when the owner caught him sneaking down the stairs one night. It's said that his spirit opens and closes doors and has been seen in the "haunted mirror" in the ladies' restroom, vanishing when the startled lady turns around.

The Loft Gallery

A haunting experience happened at the Loft Gallery in the 1990s when startled customers observed a painting fly off a wall. Then, one early morning in October 2006, an artist saw a glowing mist float through the gallery. Witnesses also report footsteps, creaking floors and doors closing when no one was there.

Puzzle Palooza Etc.

The gift/puzzle shop Puzzle Palooza Etc. is family owned and operated and features a wide variety of jigsaw puzzles for all ages, interests and ability levels. Since the shop opened, many paranormal observations have been made. A ghostly child may be haunting the site according to a local paranormal investigator.

Within weeks of the shop's grand opening, the spirit made itself known. Lights flickered off and on, but maybe it was only an electric short? Or the rainy weather? Then the internet service began cutting in and out. Still maybe the weather? But the doors opening and closing on their own? The doors and windows were closed with no discernable drafts, but then a puzzle flew off a shelf.

As strange (and dare I say otherworldly) as these events are on their own merit, stranger things were still to come. Boxes of puzzles were found stacked in front of the refrigerator door, end to end.

Experimenting with the proclivities of the spirit, a floor puzzle was laid out with a couple of pieces left to the side. The following day, a piece of the puzzle was found completed and towels were carefully placed on top of the completed pieces, as if to protect them from being disturbed.

Intrigued, the owners left another puzzle on a bench in a similar fashion. The next day, not only was the puzzle completely assembled, but it was also moved.

A paranormal investigator attempted to communicate with the reported ghost. From the recording and activity, she said the building is haunted by a seven-year-old boy named Tad who was an only child. It's not known why he still frequents this space or how he came to be here. He appears to be friendly enough but every bit as mischievous as any seven-year-old.

16

INDIAN HEAD, MARYLAND

Indian Head is a town in Charles County, Maryland. The population was reported to be 3,844 at the 2010 census. It has been the site of a naval base specializing in gun and rocket propellants since 1890. Beginning around 1900, nitrocellulose and smokeless powder was produced here at the Indian Head Powder Factory. The name of the base has varied over the years from Indian Head Proving Ground to its current designation as the Naval Support Facility, Indian Head. The base employs approximately 4,000 people.

The town of Indian Head was incorporated in 1920. It is located between the Potomac River and Mattawoman Creek. The original land grant from Cecil Calvert to Captain Thomas Cornwallis was for five thousand acres and included the two-thousand-acre Cornwallis Manor on the Potomac.

Geographically, Indian Head is located on a peninsula overlooking the Potomac River and for many years was occupied by various indigenous groups. The Algonquian-speaking Mattawoman (thought to be a subgroup of the Piscataway tribe) were the first encountered by the earliest English settlers. The newly arriving Europeans dubbed the area Indian Head. (*Head* at that time was another term for peninsula.)

During the Civil War, the site was also used by the Union army Balloon Corps to spy on Confederate troop movements across the Potomac. The Balloon Corps reached heights of five hundred feet, permitting a fifteen-mile range of view. Tethered ascents kept the balloons relatively stable but required substantial ground crews. The balloons (and the ballooners) were threatened with frequent assault from Confederate sharpshooters and artillery fire requiring men to quickly raise and lower the balloon.

Many tales of ghostly apparitions and hauntings are told here. There are reports from night-time drivers claiming a figure ran out in front of them so close that they couldn't avoid them. And then they heard the sickening thump of their tires as they crushed them. When they pull over, in dreadful fear of what they will find, the road is empty with no one to be seen.

One recent resident expressed a feeling of "weirdness" when moving into her new residence here—one in easy commuting distance to Washington, D.C. She attributed the weird feeling and creepiness of the place to the fact that it was all new to her—well, at first anyway... One night, she got the sensation that someone was watching her, and her neck hairs stood up. She tried to explain it away as she often did, until she heard her name called. A chill ran up her spine and she switched on the bedroom lights. The light stayed on that night and sleep never came. The thick blankets (pulled up to her eyes) provided little solace. Since then, she's come to some sort of terms with her apparition and doesn't think it means her any harm. She's seen many shadows—where none should be—and many voices whispering in the night.

Another former resident feels it was the spirits of both Native Americans and former slaves who haunted his past home in the form of "negative energy." There were also dark shadows and voices heard at night in this house.

One neighborhood walker described passing by an old, abandoned home on the outskirts of town. He approached the open front door and peered inside to see what he described as a "demonic presence" staring back at him. It's said that satanic rituals were once held there.

What could be the source of so many sightings and phenomena? A creepy, often foggy swamp embraces much of the river's banks here. On a dark night, the pluckiest of men might feel a tremor or two when stalking through the dark, dank woods. Some people claim Native Americans are laid to rest in the surrounding woods in unmarked graves. Have they returned for their just due? Perhaps, some of the balloon tenders didn't move fast enough and a ballooner plummeted to his death during the Civil War? The original plantation once housed many enslaved people, might they too wander in search of justice, freedom or retribution?

PART VI
TIDEWATER TO THE CHESAPEAKE BAY

THE TIDEWATER REGION OF Virginia and Maryland is a land of cultural diversity. From the old-world charm and anachronisms of the Old Order Mennonite farms in Loveville to the futuristic USN test programs scouring the skies and sending booming shockwaves through the otherwise tranquil area, it's a community in transition. In the span of a few decades, the rural heritage of the area has been transformed. Many centuries-old family farms no longer feel the caress of the self-reliant farmer's plow as housing developments and strip malls spring up to accommodate the influx of people and technology. Hardworking, independent watermen become rarer and rarer as the shorelines become dotted with the mansions of the affluent newcomers.

The land reflects its own version of diversity as well. Inland, farmers traditionally worked the land, while closer to the rivers, watermen plied their trade. Fresh-flowing creeks and rivers meet the salinity of the lower Potomac's tides, creating a brackish mix appealing to a variety of species.

Local family names, once known by all, were trusted or reviled based on their antecedents. Loyalties or feuds were solidified by centuries of shared association. This quantitative certainty gave way to new "devils or angels" unknown. The fresh wave of interlopers rocked the local inhabitants as surely as the European invasion did nearly four centuries before.

It's said it's the same everywhere, this melting pot of American culture. But few places have experienced such rapid societal change as evidenced here, nor the dramatic culture clash of dissimilar mores and backgrounds. We all cling to the familiar, the comforts of hearth and home—even as a way of life disappears. Can the current fascination with the macabre, spectral ancestors and spiritualism be our desperate attempt to reconnect with a dying way of life?

17

COLONIAL BEACH, VIRGINIA

Colonial Beach, Virginia, is a river town located in the northwestern part of Westmoreland County on what is called Virginia's Northern Neck peninsula. It is surrounded by the Potomac River, Monroe Bay and Monroe Creek. It's just over an hour's drive to Washington, D.C., and thirty-five miles from the confluence with the Chesapeake Bay.

The town was incorporated on February 25, 1892, and was a bathing and fishing resort beginning in the late nineteenth century, affectionately known as the "Playground on the Potomac." This vaunted status remained until the middle of the twentieth century, when the Chesapeake Bay Bridge (as well as increased automobile traffic) allowed easy access to more distant beaches. George Washington's birthplace is very near here on Popes Creek (less than a mile south of the creek's confluence with the Potomac River). The town is home to the second largest public sand beach in Virginia. As of 2010, there were 3,500 people residing in the town.

For a small town, there is much history here. Excavations found many Native American artifacts. Further study and the surveying of oyster pits (middens) indicate that Native Americans inhabited the area of modern-day Colonial Beach since at least the Early Woodland Period (500 BC–AD 900).

It is considered the epicenter of the Maryland/Virginia "Oyster Wars." Most sources give the dates of these hostilities as beginning in 1865 and ending in 1962, when President John F. Kennedy signed the Potomac Fisheries Bill. This act established a bistate commission to oversee the

The Bell House, Colonial Beach, Virginia. *From author's collection.*

Potomac River. Even before this time, however, a violent and competitive friction existed on the Potomac and Chesapeake waterways.

It manifested itself over three waves of tragedy and bloodied southern Maryland's waters. The conflict came to a head on April 17, 1959, when a Maryland police boat fired on a Virginia poacher's oyster boat. One of the oyster boat occupants, Berkeley Muse, yelled, "I'm hit" and slumped over the boat's culling board. The firing continued, and the boat's captain, Harvey King, was hit in the leg. Rushing to shore, Muse died before the ambulance arrived. Public outcry after the incident led to the disarming of the police force and eventually to Kennedy's Potomac Fisheries Commission. These actions effectively ended the bloody Oyster Wars.

Violence and bloodshed often beget paranormal activity, but that doesn't appear to be the case at the Bell House. The home now serves the community as a bed-and-breakfast and was once the summer residence of Alexander Graham Bell. Here, it seems likely the former (mortal) residents were so enamored of their beautiful home in its prize location on the river that they were unable, or unwilling, to move on when they felt the cold whisper of death. At the Bell House, many have reported seeing Alexander Graham Bell's father, Melville Bell, standing at the windows. They claim his flowing white hair and beard are quite distinctive.

Another visitor from beyond the veil is affectionately known as Bertha. It is supposed that she lived here for some years, judging by the antique hairpins so often found on the floor.

A few miles away, the Dockside Restaurant resides on Gum Bar Point. After the horrendous flood of 1985, the skeletal remains of several men were uncovered by the receding waters. It's thought that the skeletons were of men forced into labor aboard a seventeenth-century fishing boat. Soon thereafter, the site was nicknamed "Ghost Point." One of the ghosts here is identified only as "Charlie," who frequents the point, perhaps one of the unfortunate seamen from long ago.

18
Leonardtown, Maryland

Leonardtown is the county seat of St. Mary's County, Maryland, and has a population of approximately three thousand people. This number has soared in recent years due to the nearby Patuxent River Naval Air Station. It is also the site of the county fairgrounds, which hosts the annual national oyster-shucking championship. Historical records of the area referred to it as Newtowne or Newtowne Hundred as early as 1654. In 1660, it was incorporated as Seymour Town, named after Governor John Seymour. Nearly two decades later, it was renamed Leonard Town in honor of Governor Benedict Leonard Calvert.

During the War of 1812, more than one thousand British soldiers held the town in submission even as they blockaded the Chesapeake Bay. Residents of the town (and most of the county) were subjected to repeated plundering and malicious destruction up to and including stabling horses inside of churches and laying waste to tombstones in area graveyards.

During the Civil War, Union military units occupied Leonardtown. The mayor was arrested for pro-Confederate views and the printing press was seized. Homes were searched for weapons and supplies that were confiscated for fear they'd be transported across the Potomac to Virginia. Southern Maryland and the town's sympathies lay with the Confederacy.

Perhaps no legend is as prevalent in Leonardtown lore or more a part of the collective consciousness of the town as the story of Moll Dyer, the accused witch. After three hundred years, Moll's name is still heard here, especially around campfires late at night or as a warning to misbehaving kids. A recent film is said to have been based on her life. If so, there were many inaccuracies, the least of which was planting her in the middle of Maryland's Alleghany Mountains in lieu of the true origin of her story—the tobacco fields of southern Maryland. The Weather Channel aired a segment on her life, of course highlighting the impact of weather during colonial times. (Drought and extreme winter temperatures figure prominently in her story.)

The historical evidence of the life of the "Winter Witch" is mostly undocumented. Courthouse records from the late 1600s were destroyed in a fire. However, there's evidence of several female Dyers arriving in Maryland around this period that fit in with the legend. A letter written by a colonist references "Moll Dyer having a countenance so ugly it hurts to behold her." Further circumstantial evidence includes a road named after her and, likewise, a small run that traverses what is said to be the original Dyer homestead near Leonardtown, Maryland.

Most stories associated with Moll state that she came alone to the colony from Ireland via England, but some oral traditions hold that she was accompanied by an absentee uncle or older male family member. Many reports describe her clothing as old and threadbare but originally made of high-quality materials, such as the nobility of the era might have worn. This seeming contradiction raises many questions about her ancestry and adds to her mystery.

The legend of Moll Dyer is considerable. She was renowned for her curative prowess and hated for her lack of social graces. A virtual hermit, she traded herbal remedies with local Native Americans, and it's said that she enjoyed their companionship over that of her own people. These traits alone made the unattractive old woman suspect to the very superstitious citizenry. A two-year drought began in the late spring of 1695 and caused demoralizing crop loss. On the heels of this devastation, a disease broke out. As she was already a social pariah, the blame fell on Moll Dyer. Surely, she was a witch. And what's to be done with a witch?

Moll Dyer road sign, Leonardtown, Maryland. *From author's collection.*

The colonial governor arrived at a local gathering in the village of Newtowne (now Leonardtown, Maryland) intending to celebrate with the locals, shake hands and kiss some babies, but he ran into Moll Dyer. Exactly what transpired between them is unknown, but shortly thereafter, the governor's children became deathly ill. Searching for a cause for this and their other misfortunes, the citizens pointed their collective fingers at Moll Dyer. Proclaiming her a witch, they demanded the governor's intercession. Aware of the ignominy of Salem, Massachusetts, only four years prior, the official stated that there would be no official sanction against her, but he'd not stand in the way of their "due justice."

In the dark of the coldest winter night of 1697, a frenzied mob of God-fearing colonists rose up against her, determined to see righteousness restored to the colony. Armed with flintlock rifles, pitchforks and axes, they set out for Moll's cabin, their way lit by many blazing pine knots. It's not known who threw the first torch, but in mere moments, fire devoured the dry wooden structure. Somehow, Moll escaped her intended funeral pyre through a back door and fled blindly through the woods.

Several days later, a young lad was searching for his missing cow. He stumbled upon Moll's lifeless body bent over a large rock at the river's edge, frozen solid. When Moll was wrenched away, the rock bore indentations where one palm had rested and her knees touched. One arm was frozen in an upright position, some say in entreaty to a higher power, some say to complete the curse on her tormentors. The latter reasoning held sway on the populace. They concluded that the power of her witchcraft engraved the marks in the stone, cursing the land and her killers.

MOLL'S ROCK

3 Notch Paranormal Investigations recently checked out Moll's famous (infamous?) rock. Their discoveries and experiences were recorded and revealed on their YouTube channel, Haunted Southern Maryland. At one point in the video, the investigators are receiving responses to questions on their EVP and ask the spirit to show themself. Shivers run down this viewer's spine as a female figure's distinct electronic image is seen reclining over Moll's rock.

The eight-hundred-pound rock sat for many years in the courtyard of the Saint Mary's County Courthouse with a simple plaque proclaiming it as "Moll Dyer's Rock, Circa 1697." Curious visitors to southern Maryland report both curses and cures after touching the infamous rock. Perhaps it

Moll Dyer's Rock, Leonardtown, Maryland. *From author's collection.*

depends on how the individual interprets Moll's story, or could it be that Moll remembers their ancestor among those wielding a flaming torch on that fateful night?

Over the years, many reputable eyewitnesses have reported seeing the ghostly white figures of a woman and her wolfish dog spiriting through the mists along the small creek that bears Moll's name. Many photography buffs have snapped pictures of the apparitions and of the small stream, only to later discover that no image was preserved. Hikers, hunters and other strong-willed and rational people have scurried away from these sightings, unashamed of their fear but reticent to share their encounters. Some of the residents of the area near Moll's old homestead have reported engines shutting down or the electrical components on their ATVs going crazy. One prior resident stated that he's been awakened at night by the sounds of a mob and baying hounds—but when investigated, no one was to be seen. Wide-eyed drivers in numerous automobile accidents bear witness to the bizarre sights they claim distracted them. It is interesting to read those police reports.

After dozens of interviews with local families—families resident to the area since the time of Moll Dyer—it's soon learned that each has their own version of Moll's life, but with minimal variations. As there is a dearth of historical records, it is toward these legends we must focus our efforts. (According to the Archives of Maryland, the first loss of St. Mary's County records was in 1768 when records kept at the home of Owen Alien, or Allen, were burned. The archive notes this only as an FYI, as "every surviving court record of the period [colonial] was destroyed in the fire of March 8, 1831.") To add to the confusion and speculative nature of the search, Ancestry.com lists five pages of Dyers on passenger lists arriving in the United States during the period, a minimum of six Mary or Margaret Dyers. It goes on to state that "lists were not kept for every ship" (perhaps less than half) and many records have been lost. (The endearment "Moll," by the way, was most commonly used as a nickname for Mary but was also occasionally seen for any *M* feminine name including but not limited to Margaret, Martha, Martina and Melinda.)

What can we derive from the legends associated with Moll Dyer? Although there are some small deviations to the legend, the majority of local families' oral traditions agree: she was an herbal healer and hermit. Most state her origin was Ireland, although she likely arrived on a passenger ship from England. She arrived on our shores a single woman and never married. She preferred the company of the Native Americans to her European neighbors. She dressed in a manner of lost affluence (threadbare clothes originally made from the finest materials). She froze to death on the coldest night of 1697 after a citizen mob burned her small cabin to the ground. (With this information, the novel *Sister Witch: The Life of Moll Dyer*, incorporated all reported variations of the story. It would be unfaithful to her memory, legend and life to have done otherwise.)

So then, who is/was Moll Dyer? I won't fabricate a correlation between any segment of the legend and other past lives lived here. It's unnecessary to make her story more real. Her tragedy speaks to its own truth, and perhaps that's enough. My answer to the question is Moll's truth, even if intangible.

Moll Dyer is everyone who's faced injustice or been mocked for being different—those scorned for their beliefs and tormented for living a life true to themselves. She is anyone condemned at the court of public opinion and castigated for their lack of popularity or political correctness. She's the embodiment of Sarah Goode of Salem fame, Anne Frank, John the Baptist, Joan of Arc, Anne Boleyn, Rosa Parks and the list goes on and on. Moll could be the patron saint of them all.

In conclusion, I believe Moll Dyer would be proud of her legacy and that she'd feel some measure of peace and exoneration from the tales being told of her today. She was once used as a cautionary tale—a warning to little children to behave, but no longer. Now we remember Moll whenever we're bullied, accused without cause or feeling friendless. Perhaps she gives us a twinge of conscience when we are the ones doing the bullying? It warms my heart to think so—that some good is our final inheritance from the tragedy of Moll Dyer.

Moll Dyer's Rock is an important and popular attraction in southern Maryland. It has resided in front of the old jail (now a museum) since 1972 after its discovery by Philip Love in 1968. In February 2021, the Saint Mary's County Historical Society moved this memorial to its new home at Tudor Hall in Leonardtown, including an engaging and well-received dedication ceremony. The rock was placed in a location available to the public with protection from the elements in an effort to preserve the sandstone "monument" for future generations.

Other notable hauntings in the Leonardtown area have been investigated by the 3 Notch Paranormal Investigations team. These sleuths and afficionados of the invisible world—Jeannie and Tracy, along with videographers Chay and Courtney and audio tech Philip—are confident that one law office in Leonardtown is most assuredly haunted. Non-believers have reconsidered their stance after hearing energetic typing sounds in an otherwise empty building. The beeping sounds associated with a computer waking up have been heard by multiple witnesses when all computer screens remained dark. Perhaps something else was awakened? The name "Edison" has been heard using EVP recordings, although there's no known history of anyone by that name associated with the building. A shadow man described as a tall dark figure occasionally makes his presence known appearing out of nowhere to take a jaunt down the hall and through the walls. A very old antique desk decorates one office space and is thought to be the focus of some of the paranormal activity in that section of the building.

A very old cemetery (located appropriately enough on Cemetery Road) is a site of some interest. This is the old St. Aloysius Gonzaga Cemetery (circa 1766) that was started by Reverend James Walton. Five Confederate soldiers are buried here, and it was at these soldiers' graves that the paranormal researchers focused their efforts. Several gravesites exhibited some degree of activity, particularly those of John Francis Duke, Duncan Turner and

Vincent Camalier. At Duke's grave, excerpts from Robert Long's book *Valor in a Border State* were read aloud. The entry described Duke's capture and imprisonment at Point Lookout and one of the family's stories about Duke was included. It held that as he was walking home to Leonardtown upon his release, a Yankee troop wagon stopped and asked Duke if he would like a ride. Duke replied, "I would rather crawl home on my hands and knees than ride with you Yankees." It would seem this reading stirred deeply held memories for Duke—even in the afterlife. Shortly after, a compelling photo was taken showing a dark figure standing in front of his grave—though no mortal beings were in that area. His headstone glowed with an ethereal light, though only a handful of votive candles added any nonambient light.

If you find yourself in the most haunted county in Maryland, take a drive by Moll Dyer Road and take a glance at Moll Dyer's Run on your way to the old courthouse and Tudor Hall in Leonardtown. Once there, if you're the adventurous sort, check out Moll's Rock. Does it initiate curses or cures? Could it depend on the mood of her spirit? Or is it the content of the visitor's heart? Give Moll's Rock a rub to find out for yourself—if you dare.

19
Piney Point, Maryland

Piney Point Lighthouse is a creation of the famed lighthouse builder John Donahoo using a conical stone tower. The lighthouse is thirty-five feet tall and included a lighthouse keeper's quarters built separate from the tower. In 1836, the design was completed, and the light flickered to life for the first time.

The lighthouse was located fourteen miles north of the Potomac's confluence with the Chesapeake Bay. Its location made it an ideal getaway from the stresses of city life, and it soon became known as the "President's light house." Teddy Roosevelt, Franklin Pierce and James Monroe were all known to have relaxed in the shade of the tower and fished the waters of the Potomac here.

Sadly, the lighthouse was decommissioned in 1964, but its saga continued. Taken over by the Saint Mary's County Recreation and Parks in 1990, it is now open to the public. Since its opening, it's been turned into a veritable cornucopia for curious mariners, military fans, lighthouse lovers and history aficionados. During World War II, a German U-boat, called a Black Panther, was captured and eventually towed to Piney Point to be sunk. The U-1105 submarine now serves as Maryland's first historic shipwreck dive preserve.

Over the years, many possible hauntings have been reported, including construction workers repairing the old structures. They recounted hearing disembodied voices that frequently distracted their efforts. Others have described the same, and a paranormal group called the D.C. Hauntings Paranormal Group investigated. Oddly, they never released their findings, and I fear they are now defunct. I can find no current references to them. Did they hear Germanic orders barked at crewman they couldn't see? It's said that disembodied spirits return to the scene of their greatest triumphs, especially if their later years were lived in shame. Is there a more likely candidate than that engendered by the saga of the U-boats and their sailors? Perhaps the investigators recorded the cries of wrecked seaman from the days before the lighthouse safely lit their way? Or maybe they heard nothing at all.

During my visit to the lighthouse, I heard no spectral voices, but I will confess to feeling odd, especially as I walked around the base of the lighthouse keeper's house. My recorder picked up no verifiable EVPs, but there were sounds I could not readily identify. I attributed this strange feeling to being alone in the presence of history—a place where many have lived, loved, labored and died.

The surrounding park and museum boast many activities to draw your interest—notwithstanding the ghostly elements. You can climb the oldest lighthouse on the Potomac, see their many restored historic boats and learn some maritime history in the museum. Offshore, the sunken World War II–era U1105 (U-boat) is a Historic Shipwreck Dive Preserve. Stop by and take a walk on the beach, launch your kayak or bring a picnic lunch. Even though the ghosts seldom pester a daytime visitor, keep an eye out just in case.

20
Saint George's Island, Maryland

St. George's Island is an unincorporated area in Saint Mary's County, Maryland, and was founded in 1634. It overlooks the confluence of Saint Mary's River and the Potomac. The post office located at Piney Point, Maryland, serves the island, with a short span of bridge connecting it to the mainland.

In July 1776, the first battle of the Revolutionary War on Maryland soil occurred here. During the War of 1812, the British made the island their headquarters and raided shipyards and river plantations from this base. Much lumber from the virgin forests was cut from the island and shipped to England for ship masts. In the nineteenth century, the Roman Catholic Church, which owned the island, finally opened it to settlement.

Of interest to this narrative is a haunt that dates to the War of 1812. It is said that the island was used as a huge burial plot by the British to lay their lost sailors and soldiers to rest. Uncounted numbers of bodies were reportedly buried here. Most were scattered about the island, but one mass grave was used during a particularly bloody period of the war. The burial site remained perfectly circular and devoid of vegetation through the years. I was unable to identify the exact spot where the Devil's Ball Yard is found, due to the island's erosion and the rising waters of the Potomac, but I believe it to be a marshy area above a small beach on the river.

Ever since the entombment, ghostly spectacles have been reported here. The nickname of the site derives from the local tale. It's said that the devil

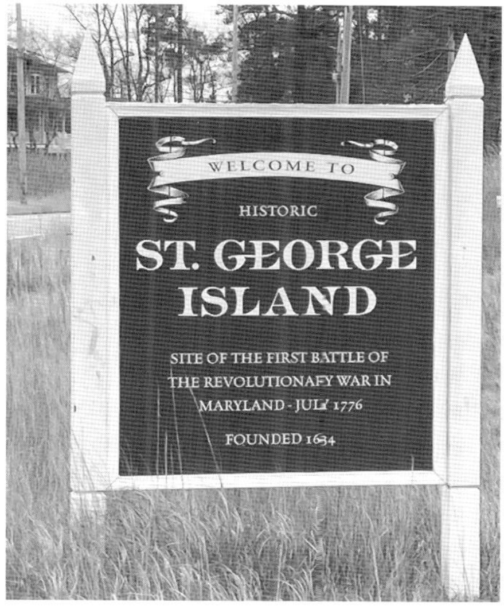

Left: War of 1812, Saint George's Island, Maryland. *From the author's collection.*

Right: Welcome to Saint George's Island, Maryland. *From the author's collection.*

Possibly the elusive Devil's Ball Yard, Saint George's Island, Maryland. *From the author's collection.*

himself perpetuates the smooth round burial site by holding monthly balls above the dead buried there. The demonic dancers have been reported "floating" across the Potomac and the surrounding woods, shadow-beings intent on attending the monthly ghoulish festivities ordered by their dark lord.

None of the reticent interviewees had observed the actual devil's ball, but one admitted to seeing the dark figures moving toward them across the river. The recollection of the night still made their voice quiver and skin crawl when relating the tale. Some swore to never go back. None stayed to verify the hellish frivolity to follow or asked for their own invitation.

21
SAINT MARY'S CITY, MARYLAND

Saint Mary's City is strategically located just before the confluence of the Saint Mary's River and the mighty Potomac. It is the site of the first European settlement in the new Maryland colony in 1634 and of the state's first capital. It remained the capital until displaced by Annapolis in 1783 (then called Anne Arundel Town). Saint Mary's City was declared a National Historic Landmark in 1969 and is a well-known archaeological site. Along with a multitude of colonial artifacts are many from the Woodland Indian period and earlier. Recently, three lead coffins were unearthed here, thought to belong to members of the Calvert family. One is considered to be that of Philip Calvert, a colonial chancellor and judge. Lead coffins are a rare find for the time period and speak to considerable wealth.

Both the re-created historic site and the adjacent Saint Mary's College are prime paranormal spots. Included in the reconstruction efforts is a Native village built to reflect the technology of the period. There have been reports of a Yaocomico brave (the tribe is a subgroup of the Piscataway tribe) seen on several occasions roaming nearby trails. Observers have followed him, thinking him to be one of the reenactors who work there, only to have the young brave disappear on the trail in front of them. I guess he feels at home in the shadow of the longhouse resembling that of his people from centuries past.

Spirits attired in seventeenth-century garb make frequent appearances. Like the Yaocomico brave, they're spotted along the deserted trails moving to and from the different sections of their town.

Native American–style dwelling at historic Saint Mary's City, Maryland. *From author's collection.*

Replica of the Maryland Dove. One of two vessels (*Ark* and *Dove*) that brought original colonists to Maryland. Historic Saint Mary's City. *From author's collection.*

If you decide to explore the grounds—and you should—enjoy the living history reenactments, the accurate reproduction of the *Dove* (the *Ark* and the *Dove* were the two ships that brought the original colonists to these shores) and a museum full of period historical displays. A side trip to the Inn at Brome Howard (a renovated 1840s inn) might be in order. It's listed as a National Historic Landmark. As such, its history is long and complex. Perhaps a spirit or two resides there as well?

22
SCOTLAND, MARYLAND

Scotland, Maryland is located in St. Mary's County, a small unincorporated community near the southernmost end of the state on the western shore of the Chesapeake Bay. Located here is a summer camp operated by the Metropolitan Police Department and the Greater Washington Area Boys and Girls Club. Also located here is Point Lookout, the former site of a Civil War prison camp, the Point Lookout Confederate Cemetery and Point Lookout State Park.

POINT LOOKOUT PRISON CAMP

From the lighthouse to the prison camp and everywhere in between, Point Lookout is the most haunted site in Maryland, if not the entire country, rivaling Gettysburg, Pennsylvania, for this dubious distinction. Its haunted history is even noted on state-sanctioned brochures and webpages, a rare nod to the paranormal by any governmental body.

Named during the War of 1812 for providing a watch post for British invaders, this narrow strip of land marks the southernmost point of the western shore of Maryland. It's formed by the confluence of the Potomac River with the Chesapeake Bay, giving it great value for fishermen, traders, vacationers and, of course, warmongers. Indian massacres, lighthouse deaths, shipwrecks, multiple suicides and the barbaric hospital and camp conditions during the Civil War period have amassed a large population of spectral residents. The POW camp provides the most fodder for the paranormal mill, and a large percentage of the hauntings date to this period.

In the course of the war, 52,264 Confederate soldiers were incarcerated here at Fort Lincoln's Camp Hoffman. Many died of dysentery, typhoid fever, malaria, smallpox, starvation and murder. The exact number of deaths is impossible to pinpoint, as many soldiers were entombed in mass graves during periods of high mortality. One such period was in May 1865 (three months after the war's end), when 324 men died in the thirty-one-day span.

Barracks were not provided for the inmates, only a sunken tent city nicknamed the "bullpen." Up to sixteen men were assigned to each fifteen-square-foot tent, with one blanket to share among every three men. Rations were starvation diets, and many inmates depended on rats for their source of protein.

Animosity was to be expected from wartime enemies, but Point Lookout was regarded as one of the cruelest camps, although not as popularized as Andersonville. Included among the guards were United States Colored Troop (USCT) Regiments, but the brutality wasn't confined to the former slaves. In fact, many were stunned by the conditions their former enslavers were forced to endure. One former captive wrote that officers of the day often offered ten to fifteen dollars to guards for each prisoner they shot in "the discharge of their duties" that day.

Park maintenance program supervisor Greg Knott has observed some of Point Lookout's secrets for himself. He tells of the maintenance building that was erected in the area of the prison pen. Late at night, footsteps can often be heard moving up and down the stairs. The slamming of doors is heard when no other person is occupying the building.

Once, he spotted the mysterious Civil War–era lady. Dressed in period clothing with a wide-brimmed hat, she walked across the road from the pen area toward the water. He'd seen no vehicle and wondered where she originated from. There's only one road in, and that comes to a dead-end circle at the point. He drove to the end and circled back to pass by where he'd first spotted her. He saw no one and no vehicle. Moving on, he met another park employee driving toward him. He stopped her and asked if she'd seen a vehicle—or the woman—but she stated that the entire park was empty and no vehicles had made their way past her.

The maintenance supervisor, his curiosity piqued, turned the vehicle around to retrace his route. Approaching the area, he spotted the woman silhouetted in the open area near the water. He turned his vehicle down one

Civil War Memorial. Point Lookout, Maryland. *From the author's collection.*

of the employee-only access roads that led to the spot, the trees blocking his view of her for but a moment, and she was gone. Park rangers and longtime park visitors call the spectral lady Misses Courtney, and she is thought to be someone who once lived at the point—likely before the war.

Many other ghosts are reported from this period. A one-armed Confederate soldier searches for his brother, while others hunt for their grave sites. One soldier is often seen crossing the road from the site of the smallpox quarantine unit. His homespun uniform is in tatters, and as he passes, the scents of gunpowder and mildew assail the nostrils of the living. This spirit does not speak and appears to be unaware of observers as he continues on his way toward the river and anticipated liberty. It's doubtful he made it to freedom during his lifetime. Towers with armed guards were strategically placed around the camp, and an iron-clad warship, the USS *Roanoke*, guarded against any escape via the water. Despite the fact that the camp was surrounded by Confederate sympathizers, there were only fifty successful escapes.

Death from disease was commonplace at the prison. So much so that it was normal procedure for nurses in the smallpox quarantine hospital to pinch patients' toes to determine if they were alive. Many overnight campers in recent years have been jerked awake in the middle of the night when their toes are pinched by unseen fingers through their sleeping bags.

Along with the many sightings, electronic voice phenomena (EVP) have been recorded on the road leading from the river to the camp. These voices are reported saying, "He's in bad shape" and "fire if they get too close to you." But most of the ethereal figures remain silent when encountering the living. Perhaps their anguish requires silent reflection, or maybe what they witnessed is beyond the scope of human exchange—whether dead or alive.

POINT LOOKOUT LIGHTHOUSE

In 1830, the Point Lookout Lighthouse was built in the aftermath of generations of shipwrecks. The energies of several Civil War soldiers, lighthouse keepers of old and sailors predating the North–South conflict frequent the building and surrounding area. With some regret, I found that, as of this writing, the lighthouse is closed to the public while safety concerns are addressed and renovations made.

The site has been investigated by several paranormal television shows and, in 1980, by Doctor Han Holzer, a prominent paranormal researcher. Here the team found great success in recording EVP. Twenty-four separate vocalizations were picked up, including the following. "This is my house," ascribed to Ann Davis, former lighthouse keeper and the first woman to receive an official keeper's appointment on the Chesapeake Bay. She was found dead in the lantern room after having completed her daily routine.

Other, less readily identifiable ghosts, were recorded saying, "I was in the water." In another instance, a woman's voice suggested, "Let's take no objection to what they are doing." One voice pleaded, "Help us," and, later, a gruff older man's voice commanded, "Get off that pier." Sadly, a young child is heard to ask, "Can I play?" Several visitors to the lighthouse have reported the sound of pounding horse hooves approaching, but no spectral horses were seen by anyone I interviewed.

Visual phenomena are also well documented here. There's the man who stands silent on the lighthouse porch and then walks into the wall and disappears when spoken to. A young lad, estimated to be about eight years old, has been seen. He's known to interact with visitors. Is it conceivable that he's the same boy who asks to play? On the beach fronting the lighthouse, multiple figures have been seen walking along the sand. They abruptly disappear when lights from vehicles or flashlights attempt to illuminate them.

The 3 Notch Paranormal Investigators spent several evenings documenting the spectral happenings at this very haunted site. There they heard what many have reported—ghostly footsteps ascending to the lighthouse's cupola. They were brave enough to chase after the intruder or restless spirit but found no one there. On another occasion, video captured two orbs chasing each other. The camera followed their movements across the room and up the stairs where a second camera picked them up as they made the turn around the second landing to continue on their way.

Program supervisor Greg Knott shared some personal experiences he's had in and around the site. After Hurricane Irene raked the shores of the bay, the basement of the lighthouse flooded. As the water receded, he and another park employee entered the basement to evaluate the damage from its only access point, the interior steps. Although the water was gone, it left behind a fine, muddy silt covering the floor. Ten feet from the bottom step, they saw a series of disturbances in the mud and investigated. Footprints began, I reiterate, a full ten feet from the stairway. Such a jump would qualify for the Olympics, and the effort would have left sign of a slip at the muddy landing, but that wasn't the case. The footprints continued from there across the floor until the midpoint of the room, where they disappeared again, as if the walker levitated through the floor joists above.

One of the last residents in the lighthouse was Laura Berg in the 1970s. Accepting the presence of the spirits sharing her domicile, she felt no fear and never considered that they meant her any harm. In fact, she suspected that the spirit of Ann Davis might have saved her life.

Point Lookout Lighthouse, Point Lookout, Maryland. *From the author's collection.*

One night as she slept peacefully, she woke to see lights dancing above her bed. She felt an abiding sense of dread and danger, followed by a strong smoke smell. She fled her bedchambers and descended to the lower level of the lighthouse and found a space heater engulfed in flames. Arriving before the flames spread, she smothered the fire in short order. Without the timely warning, however, she felt the outcome would've been devastating.

One notable apparition not falling in the Civil War timeframe is thought to be Joseph Heaney (Haney), the second mate of the cargo and passenger ship *Express* out of Baltimore. Unaware of the severe storm warnings, the steamer ship met up with a coastal storm (named the Gale of '78). The severe winds ripped the deck off Heaney's ship, and waves ripped it to pieces off Point Lookout. Sixteen lives were lost, including Heaney's.

Local oral tradition holds that Heaney attempted to gain shore via rowboat for assistance from the lighthouse keeper, but because of the raging storm, he never made it to land. But that wasn't the last that was seen of him.

During severe storms, he's been heard knocking at the door of the lighthouse. On occasion, he's appeared on the beach in a sopping wet period uniform just before severe weather strikes, perhaps to warn unsuspecting sailors of the imminent storm.

On January 11, 1966, an era ended when the lighthouse's light was extinguished for the last time—but it seems some of the former residents never left.

POINT LOOKOUT OVERLOOKS THE final push of the Potomac River to its confluence with the Chesapeake Bay. It also marks the last of our tales of the Haunted Potomac River valley.

THE END

BIBLIOGRAPHY

The material in this book has been drawn from many sources, both published and online. As a native "born and bred" southern Marylander and devoted "river rat," most of these tales are familiar from conversations with other locals over the course of a lifetime. These are the oral traditions of longtime residents and the experiences and recollections of them and their families. These were their times and places—their echoes of the past.

The below referenced sources served as refreshers of these conversations and memories and fleshed out portions of the stories I was less familiar with. I've included historical facts in every case, but of course, the subject matter and the testimony of witnesses can be very subjective…

Web Pages

"Arlington County, Virginia." Wikipedia. https://en.wikipedia.org/wiki/Arlington_County,_Virginia.

Barkley, Kristin Harty. *Cumberland Times-News*, October 29, 2010. https://www.times-news.com/.

"Entler-Weltzheimer House." Historic Shepherdstown & Museum. http://historicshepherdstown.com/2015/12/10-entler-weltzheimer-house.

"Expansion of Mount Vernon's Mansion." George Washington's Mount Vernon. https://www.mountvernon.org/the-estate-gardens/the-mansion/expansion-of-mount-vernons-mansion/.

"Harpers Ferry, West Virginia." Wikipedia. https://en.wikipedia.org/wiki/Harpers_Ferry,_West_Virginia.

Ingram, David Lee. "History of the Fairfax Line." Fairfax Line. http://www.surveyhistory.org/the_fairfax_line1.htm.

"Leonardtown, Maryland Historic Information." Southern Maryland Online. http://somd.com/.

Leon, Rachel. "Puzzle Palooza Owner Reports Possible Ghostly Presence in Occoquan." Patch. May 29, 2013. https://patch.com/virginia/lakeridge/puzzle-palooza-owner-reports-possible-ghostly-presenc7b72fb33fb.

"Maryland Indian Head Ghost Sightings." Ghosts of America. http://www.ghostsofamerica.com/2/Maryland_Indian_Head_ghost_sightings7.html.

McClellan, Laurie. "5 Historic Ghost Tours." *Arlington Magazine*, October 1, 2018. https://www.arlingtonmagazine.com/5-historic-ghost-tours/.

"Old Hampshire County Jail." Haunted Places. https://www.hauntedplaces.org/item/old-hampshire-county-jail/.

"Romney, West Virginia Ghost Sightings." Ghosts of America. http://www.ghostsofamerica.com/2/West_Virginia_Romney_ghost_sightings2.html.

"Romney, West Virginia." Wikipedia. https://en.wikipedia.org/wiki/Romney,_West_Virginia.

Schmalbruch, Sarah. "The 10 Most-Visited Cities in the US This Year." Insider. December 15, 2017. https://www.insider.com/most-visited-us-cities-2017-12.

"Sharpsburg." Wiki Voyage. https://en.wikivoyage.org/wiki/Sharpsburg#Q754473.

South Atlantic Coastal Plain. https://web.archive.org/web/20090424093048/http://www.blm.gov/wildlife/pl_03sum.htm.

"Sterling, Virginia Ghost Sightings." Ghost of America. http://www.ghostsofamerica.com/2/Virginia_Sterling_ghost_sightings.html.

Walker, Jordan. "Rediscover Haunted Arlington." Arlington Public Library. October 28, 2019. https://library.arlingtonva.us/2019/10/28/rediscover-haunted-arlington/.

Walton, Geri. "Cholera and Its Suggested Remedies in the Mid 1800s." *Geri Walton* (blog). October 6, 2017. https://www.geriwalton.com/cholera-and-its-suggested-remedies-in-the-mid-1800s/.

"Washington, D.C." Wikipedia. https://en.wikipedia.org/wiki/Washington,_D.C.

"Why Some Folks Call This 'The Most Haunted Town in America." West Virginia Tourism Office. October 2017. https://wvtourism.com/most-haunted-town-shepherdstown/.

Miscellaneous

Apkarian-Russell, Pamela. *Washington's Haunted Past: Capital Ghosts of America*. Charleston, SC: The History Press, 2006.

Burnham, William J., Mary K. Burnham and Bill Burnham. *Rediscovering America: Exploring the Small Towns of Virginia and Maryland*. Winston-Salem, NC: Hunter Publishing, 2003.

Cosgrove-Mather, Bootie. "Haunted House on The Hill." CBS News. October 31, 2003.

Holzer, Hans. *Hans Holzer's Haunted America*. Wheaton, IL: Barnes & Noble Books, 1993.

LaPorte, Peter. "The Rock Is Moving." *Tudor Hall Times*, January 2021.

Michaels, Denver. *Wild & Wonderful (and Paranormal) West Virginia*. N.p.: Amazon, 2017.

Norman, Michael, and Beth Scott. *Historic Haunted America*. New York: Macmillan, 2007.

Parks, Lillian Rogers. *My Thirty Years Backstairs at the White House*. New York: Fleet Publishing, 1961.

Thompson, David W. *Haunted Southern Maryland*. Charleston, SC: The History Press, 2019.

Thomsen, Brian M. *Oval Office Occult: True Stories of White House Weirdness*. Kansas City, MO: Andrews McMeel Publishing, 2008.

Varhola, Michael J., and Michael H. Varhola. *Ghosthunting Maryland*. Cincinnati, OH: Clerisy Press, 2009.

Wilson, Sandi. "The Blonde in Black." In *Chesapeake Crimes II*, edited by Donna Andrews and Maria Y. Lima. Atglen, PA: Cornell Maritime Press, 2006.

Wilstach, Paul. *Potomac Landings*. Garden City, NJ: Doubleday, 1920.

About the Author

David W. Thompson has lived most of his life near the banks of the "Nation's River." The area written about here and the tales described are well known to him. David is the author of several historical fiction books and especially enjoys researching and writing paranormal history.

His first book in the Legends of the Family Dyer trilogy is *Sister Witch: The Life of Moll Dyer*, a historically accurate portrayal of the time period and the daily lives of the Maryland colony during the late 1600s flavored with paranormal seasoning. The second in the series is *His Father's Blood*. It traces the southern Maryland to Kentucky migration of 1785 and the lives and times of both groups. It includes many of the fables and legends associated with those times and places. The last entry in the trilogy is *Sons and Brothers*. It's set in the modern era and reunites the family—from the mountains of West Virginia to the southern Maryland coast (and, of course, Moll Dyer makes a cameo appearance). David is both appreciative and humbled by the numerous awards won by this series.

'Possum Stew is his award-winning short story collection that follows the holidays throughout the year. His novella *Call of the Falconer* is a dystopian end-of-times tale set in the not-so-distant future.

This title is the author's second book published through Arcadia Publishing and The History Press for their Haunted America imprint. The first is *Haunted Southern Maryland*, which was released on September 9, 2019.

The author enjoys kayaking on the flat-water rivers near home, as well as the more vigorous waterways in the mountains he also loves. These times afloat are his favorite moments spent with his wife and family.

His other creative pursuit is wood carving, for which he's received awards. He's a gardener (but lacks his father's expertise and devotion) and an amateur winemaker. He uses homegrown native fruits—elderberry, persimmon and Maryland's largest indigenous fruit, pawpaw.

Dave is a member of Maryland Writer's Association and the St. Mary's County Historical Society. He's easy to find on social media at:

https://www.dthompsonwrites.com
https://twitter.com/Thompson_DavidW
https://www.facebook.com/AuthorOfParanormal
https://www.goodreads.com/author/show/15425511.David_W_Thompson
https://www.amazon.com/dp/B076KR626G
Instagram @thompsondavidw